Common Core Connections
Math

Grade 4

Carson-Dellosa Publishing LLC
Greensboro, North Carolina

Credits
Content Editor: Heather R. Stephan
Copy Editor: Carrie D'Ascoli

Visit *carsondellosa.com* for correlations to Common Core, state, national, and Canadian provincial standards.

Carson-Dellosa Publishing LLC
PO Box 35665
Greensboro, NC 27425 USA
carsondellosa.com

07-133191151

Table of Contents

Introduction

What are the Common Core State Standards for Mathematics?

The standards are a shared set of expectations for each grade level in the area of math. They define what students should understand and be able to do. The standards are designed to be more rigorous and allow for students to justify their thinking. They reflect the knowledge that is necessary for success in college and beyond.

The following are Mathematical Practices as outlined in the Common Core State Standards.
1. Make sense of problems and persevere in solving them.
2. Reason abstractly and quantitatively.
3. Construct viable arguments and critique the reasoning of others.
4. Model with mathematics.
5. Use appropriate tools strategically.
6. Attend to precision.
7. Look for and make use of structure.
8. Look for and express regularity in repeated reasoning.*

How to Use This Book

The book is a collection of practice pages aligned to the Common Core State Standards for Mathematics as appropriate for Kindergarten. Included is an alignment matrix so that you can see exactly which standard is addressed on each page. Also included are a Diagnostic Test and Diagnostic Test Analysis. The assessment can be used at the beginning of the year or at any time of year you wish to assess your students' mastery of certain standards. The analysis connects each test item to a practice page or set of practice pages so that you can review skills with students who miss certain items.

Common Core State Standards*
Alignment Matrix

Pages	12	13	14	15	16	17	18	19	20	21	22	23	24	25	26	27	28	29	30	31	32	33	34	35	36	37	38	39	40	41	42	43	44	45	46	47	48	49	50	51
4.OA.1	●	●	●																																					
4.OA.2				●	●																																			
4.OA.3						●	●	●																																
4.OA.4									●	●	●																													
4.OA.5												●	●	●	●																									
4.NBT.1																●																								
4.NBT.2																	●																							
4.NBT.3																		●	●																					
4.NBT.4																					●	●	●																	
4.NBT.5																				●				●	●	●	●													
4.NBT.6																												●	●	●	●									
4.NF.1																																●	●							
4.NF.2																																			●	●	●			
4.NF.3																																						●	●	●
4.NF.3a																																						●	●	●
4.NF.3b																																								
4.NF.3c																																								
4.NF.3d																																								
4.NF.4																																								
4.NF.4a																																								
4.NF.4b																																								
4.NF.4c																																								
4.NF.5																																		●						
4.NF.6																																								
4.NF.7																																								
4.MD.1																																								
4.MD.2																																								
4.MD.3																																								
4.MD.4																																								
4.MD.5																																								
4.MD.5a																																								
4.MD.5b																																								
4.MD.6																																								
4.MD.7																																								
4.G.1																																								
4.G.2																																								
4.G.3																																								

Common Core State Standards*
Alignment Matrix

Pages	52	53	54	55	56	57	58	59	60	61	62	63	64	65	66	67	68	69	70	71	72	73	74	75	76	77	78	79	80	81	82	83	84	85	86	87	88	89	90
4.OA.1																																							
4.OA.2																																							
4.OA.3																																							
4.OA.4																																							
4.OA.5																																							
4.NBT.1																																							
4.NBT.2																																							
4.NBT.3																																							
4.NBT.4																																							
4.NBT.5																																							
4.NBT.6																																							
4.NF.1																																							
4.NF.2																																							
4.NF.3	●	●	●																																				
4.NF.3a																																							
4.NF.3b			●																																				
4.NF.3c	●	●																																					
4.NF.3d			●																																				
4.NF.4				●	●	●																																	
4.NF.4a				●																																			
4.NF.4b					●																																		
4.NF.4c						●																																	
4.NF.5																																							
4.NF.6							●	●	●	●																													
4.NF.7											●	●																											
4.MD.1													●	●	●	●	●																						
4.MD.2														●	●	●	●	●	●																				
4.MD.3																					●	●	●	●	●														
4.MD.4																								●															
4.MD.5																										●							●	●	●	●			
4.MD.5a																																							
4.MD.5b																																							
4.MD.6																										●													
4.MD.7																											●												
4.G.1																												●	●	●	●	●	●	●	●				
4.G.2																																				●			
4.G.3																																					●	●	●

After you review your student's skill assessment, match those problems answered incorrectly to the Common Core State Standards below. Pay special attention to the pages that fall into these problem sections, and ensure that your student receives supervision in these areas. In this way, your student will strengthen these skills.

Answer Key: 1. $3 \times 4 = 12$, $4 \times 3 = 12$; 2. 5; 3. 6; 4. 1, 2, 3, 4, 6, 12; 5. 11, 13, 15; 6. $700 + 70 + 7$; 7. <; 8. 60; 9. 800; 10. 643; 11. 60 words per minute; 12. 5; 13. $\frac{3}{9}$; 14. $\frac{43}{100}$; 15. <; 16. $\frac{10}{4}$; 17. $\frac{5}{9}$; 18. $5\frac{3}{4}$; 19. $2\frac{6}{9}$; 20. Check student work. 21. $2\frac{1}{3}$ and $\frac{7}{3}$; 22. $\frac{15}{4}$; 23. 9; 24. 0.6; 25. $\frac{43}{100}$; 26. 0.5, 1.5, 3.2, 3.9; 27. >; 28. 2; 29. 256; 30. 9:45 pm; 31. 72 feet; 32. 288 square inches; 33. 80°; 34. Check student work. 35. 60; 36. 70; 37. ray; 38. Student's line should form right angle with given line. 39. right; 40. Yes, Answers will vary but should include that each side of the centerline is a mirror image of the other.

Common Core State Standards*		Test Item(s)	Practice Page(s)
Operations and Algebraic Thinking			
Use the four operations with whole numbers to solve problems.	4.OA.1–4.OA.3	1–3	12–19
Gain familiarity with factors and multiples.	4.OA.4	4	20–22
Generate and analyze patterns.	4.OA.5	5	23–26
Number and Operations in Base Ten			
Generalize place value understanding for multi-digit whole numbers.	4.NBT.1–4.NBT.3	6–9	27–30
Use place value understanding and properties of operations to perform multi-digit arithmetic.	4.NBT.4–4.NBT.6	10–12	31–42
Numbers and Operations—Fractions			
Extend understanding of fraction equivalence and ordering.	4.NF.1–4.NF.2	13, 15	43–44, 46–48
Build fractions from unit fractions by applying and extending previous understandings of operations on whole numbers.	4.NF.3–4.NF.4	16–23	49–57
Understand decimal notation for fractions, and compare decimal fractions.	4.NF.5–4.NF.7	14, 24–27	45, 58–63
Measurement and Data			
Solve problems involving measurement and conversion of measurements from a larger unit to a smaller unit.	4.MD.1–4.MD.3	28–32	64–75
Geometric measurement: understand concepts of angle and measure angles.	4.MD.5–4.MD.7	33–36	77–78, 84–87
Geometry			
Draw and identify lines and angles, and classify shapes by properties of their lines and angles.	4.G.1–4.G.3	37–40	79–90

* © Copyright 2010. National Governors Association Center for Best Practices and Council of Chief State School Officers. All rights reserved.

4.OA.1

Write two multiplication facts for each fact family.

1. 5, 7, 35 _____ × _____ = _____ _____ × _____ = _____	2. 4, 6, 24 _____ × _____ = _____ _____ × _____ = _____
3. 2, 9, 18 _____ × _____ = _____ _____ × _____ = _____	4. 5, 9, 45 _____ × _____ = _____ _____ × _____ = _____
5. 8, 6, 48 _____ × _____ = _____ _____ × _____ = _____	6. 3, 8, 24 _____ × _____ = _____ _____ × _____ = _____
7. 3, 9, 27 _____ × _____ = _____ _____ × _____ = _____	8. 6, 2, 12 _____ × _____ = _____ _____ × _____ = _____

☐ I can write multiplication equations.

Use the numbers to complete two true sentences for each fact family.

1. 7, 6, 42 _____ is _____ times as many as _____. _____ is _____ times as many as _____.	2. 2, 4, 8 _____ is _____ times as many as _____. _____ is _____ times as many as _____.
3. 5, 8, 40 _____ is _____ times as many as _____. _____ is _____ times as many as _____.	4. 3, 7, 21 _____ is _____ times as many as _____. _____ is _____ times as many as _____.
5. 9, 4, 36 _____ is _____ times as many as _____. _____ is _____ times as many as _____.	6. 12, 6, 72 _____ is _____ times as many as _____. _____ is _____ times as many as _____.
7. 3, 9, 27 _____ is _____ times as many as _____. _____ is _____ times as many as _____.	8. 4, 5, 20 _____ is _____ times as many as _____. _____ is _____ times as many as _____.

☐ I understand that multiplication shows how many times a number is multiplied to get another number.

Write an equation to match each sentence. Find the answer to each equation in the bunch of balloons, and color it the matching color.

1. eight times as many as six (red)	2. seven times as many as four (blue)
3. twelve times as many as seven (green)	4. five times as many as eleven (yellow)
5. six times as many as nine (purple)	6. nine times as many as eight (orange)
7. nine times as many as three (light green)	8. seven times as many as nine (pink)

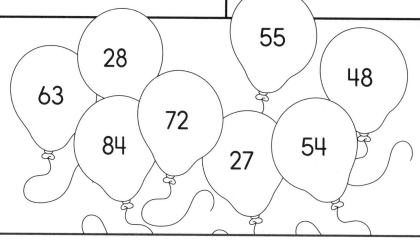

☐ I understand that multiplication shows how many times more one number is than another.

Complete the equation for each word problem. Then, find the value of the symbol.

1. There are 5 times as many frogs in Green Lake than Blue Lake. If there are 25 frogs in Green

    Lake, how many are in Blue Lake? Let 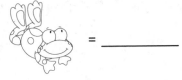 stand for the number of frogs in Blue Lake.

    25 ÷ _____ = 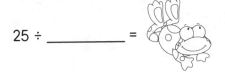   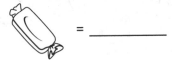 = _____

2. Jordan has 8 times as many candies as Jessica. If Jordan has 24 candies, how many does

    Jessica have? Let  stand for the number of candies Jessica has.

    _____ ×  = 24   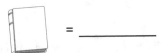 = _____

3. Julio read 10 times as many pages as Carlos. If Julio read 80 pages, how many did Carlos

    read? Let 📖 stand for the number of pages Carlos has read.

    _____ × 📖 = 80   📖 = _____

4. Madison gets 3 times the allowance that Derek gets. If Madison gets $15 per week, how much

    money does Derek get? Let  stand for Derek's allowance.

    _____ ÷ _____ = 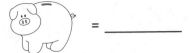   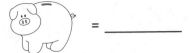 = _____

☐ I can multiply or divide to solve word problems.

Draw a picture to represent each scenario. Then, write the fact that answers the question. The first one is done for you.

1. Michael has 3 times as many clovers as Danielle. Danielle has 12 clovers.

 × 3 =

12 × 3 = 36

2. Justin has 5 times as many baseball cards as David. David has 6 cards.

3. Olivia has 16 pairs of shoes, which is twice as many as Claire.

4. Chang has 8 times as many coins as Dave. Dave has 4 coins.

5. Melanie has 21 rocks, which is 3 times as many as Jamie.

☐ I can multiply or divide to solve word problems.

Read through the story to find out how many tickets each child has. Then fill in the blank underneath each child to show their total number of tickets.

As a way to earn rewards, the students in Ms. Lindbergh's 4th grade class earn tickets for positive behavior. Elizabeth has 82 tickets, which is more than anyone else in the class. Jacob is trailing Elizabeth by 9 tickets, and Jacob has 1 more ticket than Eric. Eric has 9 times as many tickets as George but 5 fewer tickets than Emily. Claire has 3 times as many tickets as George but half as many tickets as Demetri.

Elizabeth

_____

Jacob

_____

Eric

_____

George

_____

Emily

_____

Claire

_____

Demetri

_____

☐ I can use mathematical operations and variables to solve word problems with and without remainders.

Solve each problem.

1. Elizabeth had a box of 24 crayons. Her little brother ate 2 of them, and she lost 4 of them. She split the remaining crayons between her and her 2 friends. How many crayons did each friend get?

2. Carlos's mom gave him $10 for lunch. He spent $4 on his lunch and $2 on an icecream cone, and he found $3 on the playground. How much money does Carlos have now?

3. Mrs. Chu had 20 books on the shelf in her room. The principal gave her 3 times as many to add to her shelf, and she donated 10 to the 3rd grade room. How many books does Mrs. Chu have on her shelf now?

4. Noah has a bag of jelly beans to share with his friends. The bag contains 57 jelly beans, and Noah wants to share them with 6 people. He plans to give the leftovers to his little brother. In order to split the jelly beans evenly, how many will he need to give to his brother?

☐ **I can use mathematical operations and variables to solve word problems with and without remainders.**

© Carson-Dellosa • CD-104605

Write a story problem for each picture that includes at least two operations (addition, subtraction, multiplication, or division). Then, write the equation and answer for each problem.

1.

_____

_____

_____

_____

2.

_____

_____

_____

_____

3.

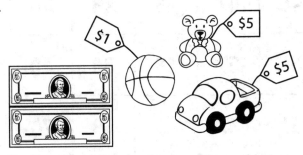

_____

_____

_____

_____

4.

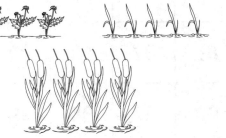

_____

_____

_____

_____

☐ I can use mathematical operations and variables to write and solve word problems with and without remainders.

Shade the squares in the grid containing the factors of each number.

1. 56   (yellow)   2. 99 (green)

3. 72   (orange)   4. 50 (blue)

1	2	3	4	5	6	7	8	9	10
11	12	13	14	15	16	17	18	19	20
21	22	23	24	25	26	27	28	29	30
31	32	33	34	35	36	37	38	39	40
41	42	43	44	45	46	47	48	49	50
51	52	53	54	55	56	57	58	59	60
61	62	63	64	65	66	67	68	69	70
71	72	73	74	75	76	77	78	79	80
81	82	83	84	85	86	87	88	89	90
91	92	93	94	95	96	97	98	99	100

☐ I can factor numbers from 1 to 100.
☐ I understand that numbers are multiples of their factors.

© Carson-Dellosa • CD-104605

Name_____

Complete each factor rainbow. The first one is done for you.

1. 24

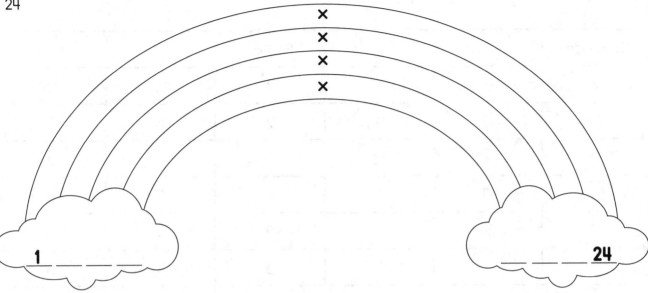

× × × ×

1 _____   _____ 24

2. 36

× × × × ×

_____   _____

In each row, cross out the factor that does not belong to the number.

Number	Factor				
1. 18	6	9	4	2	3
2. 20	10	4	2	6	5
3. 36	4	12	18	16	3
4. 52	13	21	4	2	26
5. 72	24	7	9	12	6
6. 12	1	5	3	4	6
7. 24	3	7	8	4	6
8. 50	20	2	25	50	5
9. 64	16	3	4	8	2
10. 80	5	16	8	9	20

Factor each number.

11. 30

12. 25

13. 40

14. 32

☐ **I can factor numbers from 1 to 100.**

4.OA.5

Read the number rule on each balloon. Fill in the missing numbers.

1.

Rule:
+3

0, 3, 6, 9, _____, _____, _____, _____

2.

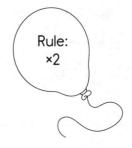

Rule:
×2

2, 4, 8, 16, _____, _____, _____, _____

3.

Rule:
+5

5, 10, 15, 20, _____, _____, _____, _____

4.

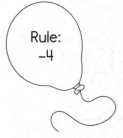

Rule:
−4

50, 46, 42, 38, _____, _____, _____, _____

5.

Rule:
+7

2, 9, 16, 23, _____, _____, _____, _____

6.

Rule:
×10

10, 100, 1,000, _____, _____, _____

7.

Rule:
+6

6, 12, 18, 24, _____, _____, _____, _____

8.

Rule:
+2

2, 4, 6, 8, _____, _____, _____, _____

☐ **I can create and describe patterns that follow a rule.**

Complete each pattern below. Then, describe the pattern for each number of blocks.

1.

Pattern: _____

2.

Pattern: _____

3.

Pattern: _____

Write your own rule for a pattern. Then, show the first 8 numbers in the pattern.

4. _____

_____

5. _____

_____

☐ I can create and describe patterns that follow a rule.

Write a rule that fits the description of each pattern. Give the first five numbers or shapes for each pattern.

1. starts at 3 and alternates between even and odd numbers without adding one

2. starts at 100, uses division, and the numbers are always even

3. starts at 3, uses multiplication, and the numbers are always odd

4. shape pattern starting with 1 block and the figure must remain square

5. starts at 2 and uses multiplication

6. shape pattern starting with 3 blocks

7. starts at 82 and uses subtraction

☐ I can create and describe patterns that follow a rule.

Write the next 3 numbers and the rule for each pattern.

1. 1, 2, 4, 7, 11, 16, 22, _____, _____, _____

   Rule: _____

2. 81, 76, 71, 66, 61, 56, 51, _____, _____, _____

   Rule: _____

3. 1, 1, 2, 2, 4, 4, 8, 8 _____, _____, _____

   Rule: _____

4. 6, 12, 22, 44, 54, 108, 118, _____, _____, _____

   Rule: _____

5. 100, 99, 97, 94, 90, 85, _____, _____, _____

   Rule: _____

6. 1, 4, 8, 11, 22, 25, _____, _____, _____

   Rule: _____

7. 5, 4, 10, 9, 15, 14, 20, _____, _____, _____

   Rule: _____

8. 9, 27, 17, 51, 41, 123, 113, _____, _____, _____

   Rule: _____

9. $\frac{1}{2}$, $\frac{5}{8}$, $\frac{3}{4}$, $\frac{7}{8}$, 1, $\frac{9}{8}$, _____, _____, _____

   Rule: _____

10. 40, 8, 80, 16, 160, 32, 320, _____, _____, _____

   Rule: _____

☐ **I can create and describe patterns that follow a rule.**

Write each number in expanded form.

1. 77

2. 357

3. 2,560

4. 459

5. 3,912

6. 1,003

Write each number in expanded form. Then, explain the relationship between the number in the ones place, tens place, and the hundreds place.

7. 88

8. 555

9. 33

10. 222

☐ I understand place value.
☐ I can explain the relationship between the numbers in the ones, tens, and hundreds places.

Write >, <, or = to compare each pair of numbers.

1. 24,064 ◯ 27,590

2. 56,000 ◯ 56,000

3. 2,641 ◯ 3,461

4. 17,048 ◯ 15,084

5. 22,728 ◯ 22,782

6. 55,491 ◯ 55,941

7. 8,463 ◯ 6,891

8. 85,485 ◯ 89,849

9. 74,912 ◯ 43,819

10. 83,214 ◯ 83,214

11. 54,295 ◯ 82,918

12. 924,146 ◯ 948,962

Order each set of numbers from least to greatest.

13. 1,408,241   9,426,597   1,400,892

_____

14. 342,192   328,191   340,384

_____

15. 68,297   405,495   929,058   65,382

_____

16. 385,722   456,817   395,024   409,990

_____

☐ I can read, write, and compare numbers up to 1,000,000.

Round the amount in each treasure chest to the nearest hundred.

1.

$692

$ _____

2.

$140

$ _____

3.

$569

$ _____

4.

$3,703

$ _____

5.

$1,684

$ _____

6.

$851

$ _____

7.

$1,456,823

$ _____

8.

$345,231

$ _____

9.

$249,999

$ _____

☐ I can round numbers up to 1,000,000.

Round to the nearest ten.

1. 72 _____

2. 55 _____

3. 14 _____

4. 62 _____

5. 83 _____

6. 17 _____

7. 49 _____

8. 29 _____

Round to the nearest hundred.

9. 284 _____

10. 924 _____

11. 561 _____

12. 354 _____

13. 752 _____

14. 728 _____

15. 689 _____

16. 192 _____

Round to the nearest thousand.

17. 1,432 _____

18. 2,418 _____

19. 1,242 _____

20. 4,299 _____

21. 6,419 _____

22. 7,546 _____

23. 9,721 _____

24. 4,142 _____

25. 5,948 _____

Round to the nearest ten thousand.

26. 23,56 _____

27. 97,453 _____

28. 12,971 _____

Round to the nearest hundred thousand.

29. 238,249 _____

30. 956,235 _____

31. 200,345 _____

☐ **I can round numbers up to 1,000,000.**

Add.

1. 37
   + 4
   ____

2. 28
   + 7
   ____

3. 56
   + 4
   ____

4. 19
   + 9
   ____

5. 73
   + 8
   ____

6. 57
   + 37
   ____

7. 66
   + 45
   ____

8. 74
   + 58
   ____

9. 98
   + 73
   ____

10. 64
    + 57
   ____

11. 348
    + 64
   ____

12. 598
    + 42
   ____

13. 198
    + 73
   ____

14. 267
    + 65
   ____

15. 667
    + 89
   ____

16. 45
     39
   + 24
   ____

17. 64
     51
   + 29
   ____

18. 88
     79
   + 53
   ____

19. 94
     48
   + 32
   ____

20. 80
     79
   + 66
   ____

Subtract.

21. 55
   – 27
   ____

22. 87
   – 48
   ____

23. 63
   – 16
   ____

24. 46
   – 28
   ____

25. 92
   – 75
   ____

26. 550
   – 16
   ____

27. 361
   – 29
   ____

28. 152
   – 19
   ____

29. 497
   – 79
   ____

30. 264
   – 28
   ____

31. 641
   – 80
   ____

32. 711
   – 84
   ____

33. 924
   – 67
   ____

34. 245
   – 84
   ____

35. 508
   – 49
   ____

☐ I can fluently add and subtract multi-digit numbers.

Solve each problem.

1. The zoo has 113 reptiles and 74 mammals. How many more reptiles than mammals does the zoo have?

2. Alex took 17 pictures of tigers, 32 pictures of birds, and 28 pictures of reptiles. How many pictures did Alex take altogether?

3. Keisha asks the zookeeper what the zoo's penguins are fed. The penguins eat 365 pounds of fish in the spring and 437 pounds of fish in the summer. How many pounds of fish do the penguins eat altogether?

4. Jason fed the bears 649 pounds of food in March. In April, Jason fed the bears 587 pounds of food. How many pounds of food did the bears eat in total?

5. Ryan counted 18 green lizards, 27 snakes, and 36 Gila monsters. How many reptiles did he see altogether?

6. On Tuesday, 1,678 people visited the zoo. On Thursday, 749 people visited the zoo. How many more people visited the zoo on Tuesday than Thursday?

7. Andrew cleaned 59 cages on Monday, 63 cages on Tuesday, and 48 cages on Wednesday. How many cages did Andy clean altogether?

8. Lisa walked 47 feet to see the leopards, 129 feet to see the alligators, and 86 feet to see the monkeys. How many feet did Lisa walk in total?

❑ I can add and subtract to solve word problems.

Add or subtract.

1. 344
    + 251

2. 467
    + 139

3. 267
    + 149

4. 3,787
    + 147

5. 6,971
    + 534

6. 2,748
    + 2,147

7. 5,471
    + 2,787

8. 4,387
    + 1,349

9. 3,661
    + 2,677

10. 28,920
    + 6,378

11. 74
    67
    + 36

12. 74
    71
    + 13

13. 73
    46
    + 27

14. 272
    156
    + 38

15. 7,514
    6,372
    + 5,401

16. 437
    24
    21
    + 13

17. 680
    71
    63
    + 14

18. 304
    41
    33
    + 17

19. 674
    341
    231
    + 143

20. 6,324
    3,641
    3,541
    + 1,032

21. 653
    – 241

22. 364
    – 192

23. 467
    – 284

24. 613
    – 267

25. 504
    – 283

26. 2,017
    – 415

27. 6,411
    – 4,254

28. 5,068
    – 2,219

29. 35,407
    – 4,761

30. 51,734
    – 2,516

❏ I can add and subtract large numbers.

Solve each problem.

1. Stuart counted 5,671 red ants. Alice counted 6,105 black ants. How many more black ants than red ants were counted?

2. The Pets-R-Us pet store sold 733 pounds of birdseed in January. In February, the store sold 559 pounds of birdseed. How many pounds of birdseed did the store sell altogether?

3. The robin flew 3,419 feet. The blue jay flew 2,866 feet. How many more feet did the robin fly than the blue jay?

4. At the butterfly exibit, Ryan saw 219 orange butterflies and 859 yellow butterflies. How many butterflies did Ryan see altogether?

5. There were 23,416 leafcutter ants in the rain forest. There were 16,980 beetles and 5,688 dragonflies. How many insects were there altogether?

6. In November, 9,717 birds flew south for the winter. Another 459 birds flew south in December. How many birds flew south altogether?

7. The garden contains 256 grasshoppers. If the garden contains 2,041 insects, how many insects are not grasshoppers?

8. Leslie saw 108 monarch butterflies in the field. Mario saw 849 monarch butterflies in the meadow. How many monarch butterflies did Leslie and Mario see altogether?

☐ I can add and subtract to solve word problems.

© Carson-Dellosa • CD-104605

Multiply.

1. 21
    × 5
    ___

2. 32
    × 3
    ___

3. 11
    × 8
    ___

4. 41
    × 2
    ___

5. 13
    × 2
    ___

6. 34
    × 2
    ___

7. 19
    × 2
    ___

8. 24
    × 3
    ___

9. 35
    × 2
    ___

10. 47
    × 2
    ___

11. 36
    × 4
    ___

12. 27
    × 4
    ___

13. 54
    × 4
    ___

14. 27
    × 6
    ___

15. 19
    × 6
    ___

16. 83
    × 7
    ___

17. 38
    × 4
    ___

18. 65
    × 4
    ___

19. 82
    × 9
    ___

20. 53
    × 7
    ___

21. 97
    × 2
    ___

22. 49
    × 4
    ___

23. 29
    × 8
    ___

24. 76
    × 5
    ___

25. 93
    × 5
    ___

26. 74
    × 6
    ___

27. 85
    × 7
    ___

28. 59
    × 3
    ___

29. 62
    × 6
    ___

30. 47
    × 4
    ___

31. 231
    × 2
    ___

32. 122
    × 3
    ___

33. 322
    × 2
    ___

34. 210
    × 4
    ___

35. 412
    × 2
    ___

36. 120
    × 3
    ___

37. 118
    × 3
    ___

38. 218
    × 2
    ___

39. 229
    × 4
    ___

40. 407
    × 2
    ___

41. 235
    × 3
    ___

42. 346
    × 2
    ___

43. 184
    × 2
    ___

44. 492
    × 2
    ___

45. 292
    × 4
    ___

46. 353
    × 2
    ___

47. 381
    × 4
    ___

48. 462
    × 3
    ___

49. 657
    × 4
    ___

50. 248
    × 6
    ___

51. 428
    × 5
    ___

52. 871
    × 3
    ___

53. 568
    × 7
    ___

54. 609
    × 4
    ___

☐ I can multiply large numbers.

Solve each problem.

1. Jan drove 843 miles. Rick drove 4 times as many miles as Jan. How many miles did Rick drive?

2. The Blueline express train traveled 5 times farther than the Redline train. The Redline traveled 643 miles. How far did the Blueline train travel?

3. Jeff drove 249 laps around the racetrack. If the racetrack is 9 miles long, how many miles did Jeff drive?

4. The flight from Cedar Junction is 4 times as many miles as the flight from Rapid City. The flight from Rapid City is 789 miles. How far is the flight from Cedar Junction?

5. Mark traveled 694 miles on his vacation. Simone traveled 3 times as many miles as Mark. How many miles did Simone travel?

6. Jack drove 129 miles on Monday and 34 miles on Tuesday. If Vanessa drove 5 times as many miles as Jack, how many miles did she drive?

7. If Amanda drove 65 miles per hour, how far did she drive in 7 hours?

8. Tony drove 543 miles farther than Paul. Paul drove 8 times as many miles as Jawan. If Jawan drove 296 miles, how far did Tony and Paul drive?

❑ I can multiply large numbers.

Name_____

Multiply.

1. 37
   × 2

2. 37
   × 12

3. 64
   × 4

4. 64
   × 34

5. 24
   × 3

6. 83
   × 24

7. 24
   × 13

8. 32
   × 24

9. 24
   × 11

10. 23
   × 18

11. 52
   × 34

12. 43
   × 24

13. 34
   × 12

14. 41
   × 31

15. 23
   × 15

16. 34
   × 21

17. 53
   × 13

18. 17
   × 12

19. 42
   × 31

20. 25
   × 14

21. 32
   × 25

22. 21
   × 17

23. 35
   × 11

24. 26
   × 13

25. 30
   × 29

26. 64
   × 17

27. 84
   × 50

28. 67
   × 15

29. 53
   × 41

30. 63
   × 19

❑ I can multiply large numbers.

Solve each problem.

1. The Cruisin' Coaster has 19 cars. If 37 people can ride in each car, how many people can ride at the same time?

2. The Jungle Adventure boats hold 14 people. If there are 24 boats, how many people can ride at the same time?

3. Harry and his friends waited 15 minutes in line for each ride. If they rode 38 rides, how many minutes did they spend waiting in line altogether?

4. Cory has 24 packages of sunflower seeds. If each package has 15 seeds, how many sunflower seeds does he have altogether?

5. Monica's yard measures 63' x 94'. How many square feet does she need to buy fertilizer for?

6. A ream of paper contains 500 sheets, and there are 10 reams in a case of paper. If Emily buys 30 cases, how many sheets of paper will she have?

7. An ant bed contains about 230 ants. If there are 6 of these beds on the playground, how many ants are there?

☐ **I can multiply large numbers.**

Name_____

Divide.

1. 4)76   2. 3)91   3. 5)86   4. 6)50   5. 2)35

6. 7)85   7. 2)49   8. 4)34   9. 8)43   10. 5)79

11. 4)312   12. 8)674   13. 3)497   14. 4)406   15. 2)677

16. 6)557   17. 3)325   18. 5)235   19. 2)407   20. 8)216

21. 3)276   22. 8)728   23. 4)108   24. 7)441   25. 5)336

☐ I can divide large numbers.

Solve each problem.

1. There are 45 reptiles at the zoo. Altogether, there are the same number of lizards, snakes, and chameleons. How many snakes are there at the zoo?

2. The Smithfield Zoo buys 7 times as much birdseed as the Parker Zoo. If the Smithfield Zoo buys 553 pounds of birdseed, how many pounds of birdseed does the Parker Zoo buy?

3. Andre feeds the penguins 249 pounds of food over 3 months. If he feeds the penguins the same amount of food each month, how many pounds of food does he feed them each month?

4. In January, 233 people visited the zoo. In February, 148 people came, and 249 people visited in March. What was the average number of people that visited the zoo each month? (Hint: Add, then divide the total by 3.)

5. Leslie sold 39 plastic animals in the souvenir shop. If each customer bought 3 animals, how many customers came into the gift shop?

6. Marcella has 140 pounds of meat. If she divides the meat between 9 cages, how many pounds of meat can she put in each cage? How much meat will be left?

7. Mark sold 145 red balloons, 348 yellow balloons, and 287 blue balloons. If each person bought 3 balloons, how many people bought balloons?

8. The zoo orders 567 pounds of fish. If the zookeeper divides the fish into 9 buckets, how many pounds of fish are in each bucket?

☐ **I can divide large numbers.**

Divide.

1. $6\overline{)497}$

2. $2\overline{)128}$

3. $5\overline{)257}$

4. $9\overline{)418}$

5. $6\overline{)678}$

6. $5\overline{)2,516}$

7. $3\overline{)8,437}$

8. $3\overline{)2,076}$

9. $8\overline{)8,179}$

10. $6\overline{)2,649}$

11. $9\overline{)5,082}$

12. $7\overline{)6,554}$

13. $5\overline{)9,479}$

14. $2\overline{)4,236}$

15. $3\overline{)6,879}$

16. $2\overline{)6,671}$

17. $4\overline{)3,424}$

18. $8\overline{)3,456}$

19. $5\overline{)9,466}$

20. $9\overline{)3,952}$

☐ I can divide large numbers.

Solve each problem.

1. Kyle is packaging jam in cartons. If each carton holds 9 bottles of jam, how many cartons will he need to package 1,934 bottles of jam?

2. Anna has 7,209 cans of soup that need to be boxed. If she puts 9 cans of soup in 1 box, how many boxes will she need?

3. Katherine has 9,315 sunflower seeds. She puts 7 seeds in each package. How many full packages of sunflower seeds does Katherine have when she is finished? How many seeds are left over?

4. Jermaine is bottling 6,488 ounces of root beer. One bottle holds 8 ounces. How many bottles will Jermaine have if he bottles all of the root beer?

5. Mario is packaging footballs in a box. Six footballs will fit in 1 box. How many boxes will Mario need if he has to package 288 footballs?

6. Katie has 2,837 flowers. If Katie puts 7 flowers in each vase, how many full vases will Katie have when she is finished?

7. Leo is bottling soda. Each bottle holds 7 ounces. How many bottles does Leo need if he has 2,786 ounces of soda to bottle?

8. Jenny is packaging fruit. She has 349 apples, 328 pears, and 548 oranges. If she puts 4 pieces of fruit in each package, how many full packages will she have when she is finished? How many pieces of fruit will be left?

☐ I can divide large numbers.

Fractions that equal the same amount are called **equivalent fractions**.

Example: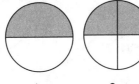

$$\frac{1}{2} \quad = \quad \frac{2}{4}$$

Write the equivalent fractions.

1. _____ = _____   2. _____ = _____   3. _____ = _____

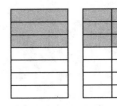

4. _____ = _____   5. _____ = _____   6. _____ = _____

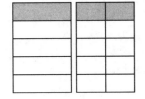

7. _____ = _____   8. _____ = _____   9. _____ = _____

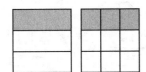

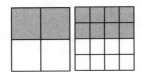

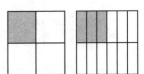

10. _____ = _____   11. _____ = _____   12. _____ = _____

☐ **I can recognize and form equivalent fractions.**

Equivalent fractions are fractions that are equal. To find equivalent fractions, multiply any fraction by 1, or by another name for the number 1. Think about it as multiplying the numerator and the denominator by the same number.

$$\frac{1}{2} \times \frac{2}{2} = \frac{2}{4} \qquad \frac{1}{2} \times \frac{3}{3} = \frac{3}{6} \qquad \frac{1}{2} \times \frac{4}{4} = \frac{4}{8}$$

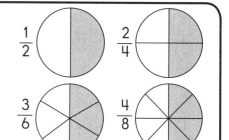

$\frac{1}{2}$ $\frac{2}{4}$

$\frac{3}{6}$ $\frac{4}{8}$

Cross out the fraction that is not equivalent to the first.

1. $\frac{1}{3}$ = $\frac{2}{6}$ $\frac{3}{9}$ $\frac{4}{8}$ $\frac{5}{15}$ $\frac{6}{18}$
2. $\frac{1}{4}$ = $\frac{2}{8}$ $\frac{3}{6}$ $\frac{4}{16}$ $\frac{5}{20}$ $\frac{6}{24}$

3. $\frac{1}{5}$ = $\frac{2}{6}$ $\frac{2}{10}$ $\frac{3}{15}$ $\frac{4}{20}$ $\frac{5}{25}$
4. $\frac{2}{3}$ = $\frac{4}{6}$ $\frac{6}{9}$ $\frac{8}{16}$ $\frac{10}{15}$ $\frac{12}{18}$

Fill in the missing number.

5. $\frac{1}{4}$ = $\frac{3}{\boxed{}}$

6. $\frac{2}{\boxed{}}$ = $\frac{4}{6}$

7. $\frac{5}{8}$ = $\frac{\boxed{}}{16}$

8. $\frac{3}{4}$ = $\frac{9}{\boxed{}}$

9. $\frac{\boxed{}}{6}$ = $\frac{2}{12}$

10. $\frac{2}{3}$ = $\frac{\boxed{}}{9}$

☐ I can recognize and form equivalent fractions.

Use equivalent fractions to rename one fraction or more in each pair. Then, add the fractions.

1. $\dfrac{4}{10} + \dfrac{8}{100}$

2. $\dfrac{3}{100} + \dfrac{7}{10}$

3. $\dfrac{1}{100} + \dfrac{9}{10}$

4. $\dfrac{3}{10} + \dfrac{7}{100}$

5. $\dfrac{9}{100} + \dfrac{9}{10}$

6. $\dfrac{11}{10} + \dfrac{11}{100}$

7. $\dfrac{2}{100} + \dfrac{3}{10}$

8. $\dfrac{5}{10} + \dfrac{7}{100}$

9. $\dfrac{2}{10} + \dfrac{3}{100} + \dfrac{1}{10}$

10. $\dfrac{5}{10} + \dfrac{7}{100} + \dfrac{5}{100}$

☐ I can add fractions with denominators of 10 and 100 by converting them into equivalent fractions.

Name_____

To compare fractions, determine which figure has more area shaded. If necessary, calculate equivalent fractions and compare the numerators.

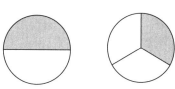

$\frac{1}{2} = \frac{3}{6}$

$\frac{1}{3} = \frac{2}{6}$

$\frac{1}{2}$ > $\frac{1}{3}$

Write a fraction for the shaded area of each figure. Then, write <, >, or = to compare each pair of fractions.

1.

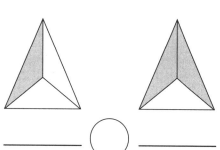

____ ◯ ____

2.

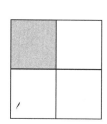

____ ◯ ____

3.

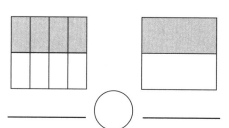

____ ◯ ____

4.

____ ◯ ____

5.

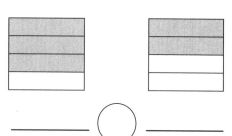

____ ◯ ____

6.

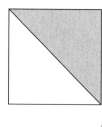

____ ◯ ____

☐ I can compare two fractions with different numerators and denominators.

46

The more parts the whole is divided into, the smaller the fraction is.

$\frac{1}{2}$		
$\frac{1}{3}$		
$\frac{1}{4}$		
$\frac{1}{5}$		
$\frac{1}{6}$		
$\frac{1}{8}$		
$\frac{1}{10}$		
$\frac{1}{12}$		

Use the fraction table to help you think about which fraction is greater. Use >, <, or = to compare each pair of fractions.

1. $\frac{1}{2}$ ◯ $\frac{1}{4}$ 2. $\frac{2}{3}$ ◯ $\frac{1}{3}$ 3. $\frac{1}{4}$ ◯ $\frac{1}{6}$ 4. $\frac{2}{6}$ ◯ $\frac{1}{3}$

5. $\frac{4}{8}$ ◯ $\frac{2}{10}$ 6. $\frac{1}{12}$ ◯ $\frac{1}{10}$ 7. $\frac{3}{4}$ ◯ $\frac{2}{8}$ 8. $\frac{2}{5}$ ◯ $\frac{1}{3}$

9. $\frac{3}{8}$ ◯ $\frac{10}{12}$ 10. $\frac{2}{8}$ ◯ $\frac{1}{4}$ 11. $\frac{1}{5}$ ◯ $\frac{2}{10}$ 12. $\frac{1}{3}$ ◯ $\frac{2}{4}$

13. $\frac{1}{6}$ ◯ $\frac{1}{3}$ 14. $\frac{3}{12}$ ◯ $\frac{1}{3}$ 15. $\frac{5}{10}$ ◯ $\frac{3}{6}$ 16. $\frac{1}{2}$ ◯ $\frac{6}{10}$

☐ I can compare two fractions with different numerators and denominators.

4.NF.2

To compare fractions, find the equivalent fractions and compare the numerators.

Example: $\frac{1}{4}$ ◯ $\frac{1}{8}$ $\frac{1}{4} = \frac{2}{8}$

$\frac{1}{8} = \frac{1}{8}$ $\frac{2}{8}$ (>) $\frac{1}{8}$ $\frac{1}{4}$ (>) $\frac{1}{8}$

Write >, <, or = to compare each pair of fractions.

1. $\frac{5}{10}$ ◯ $\frac{2}{5}$

2. $\frac{1}{6}$ ◯ $\frac{2}{3}$

3. $\frac{5}{8}$ ◯ $\frac{6}{16}$

4. $\frac{5}{10}$ ◯ $\frac{1}{2}$

5. $\frac{1}{12}$ ◯ $\frac{3}{8}$

6. $\frac{6}{7}$ ◯ $\frac{3}{21}$

7. $\frac{4}{7}$ ◯ $\frac{8}{14}$

8. $\frac{5}{12}$ ◯ $\frac{3}{4}$

9. $\frac{4}{6}$ ◯ $\frac{7}{8}$

10. $\frac{1}{7}$ ◯ $\frac{4}{21}$

11. $\frac{3}{8}$ ◯ $\frac{1}{2}$

12. $\frac{3}{6}$ ◯ $\frac{1}{18}$

13. $\frac{1}{2}$ ◯ $\frac{3}{4}$

14. $\frac{1}{6}$ ◯ $\frac{2}{12}$

15. $\frac{3}{5}$ ◯ $\frac{1}{15}$

☐ I can compare two fractions with different numerators and denominators.

Name_____

To add or subtract fractions, the denominators must be the same. To add or subtract a fraction with a common denominator, follow these steps:

1. Check that the denominators are the same.

$$\frac{3}{8} + \frac{1}{8} =$$

$$\frac{3}{8} - \frac{1}{8} =$$

2. Add or subtract the numerators. Keep the same denominator.

$$\frac{3}{8} + \frac{1}{8} = \frac{4}{8}$$

$$\frac{3}{8} - \frac{1}{8} = \frac{2}{8}$$

3. Reduce to lowest terms.

$$\frac{4 \div 4}{8 \div 4} = \frac{1}{2}$$

$$\frac{2 \div 2}{8 \div 2} = \frac{1}{4}$$

Add or subtract.

1. $\frac{2}{4} + \frac{1}{4} =$

2. $\frac{6}{8} - \frac{4}{8} =$

3. $\frac{1}{5} + \frac{3}{5} =$

4. $\frac{4}{10} + \frac{5}{10} =$

5. $\frac{7}{8} - \frac{5}{8} =$

6. $\frac{9}{10} - \frac{3}{10} =$

7. $\frac{6}{9} + \frac{2}{9} =$

8. $\frac{10}{12} - \frac{6}{12} =$

9. $\frac{15}{20} - \frac{7}{20} =$

10. $\frac{68}{100} + \frac{12}{100} =$

11. $\frac{5}{50} + \frac{15}{50} =$

12. $\frac{12}{15} - \frac{9}{15} =$

☐ I can add and subtract fractions with the same denominator.

© Carson-Dellosa • CD-104605

49

Name_____

When subtracting fractions with common denominators, follow these steps:

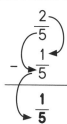

$\dfrac{2}{5}$
$-\dfrac{1}{5}$
___
$\dfrac{1}{5}$

1. Subtract the numerators.
2. Keep the same denominator.
3. Reduce to lowest terms.

$\dfrac{7}{8}$
$-\dfrac{3}{8}$
___
$\dfrac{4}{8}$ = $\dfrac{1}{2}$

Subtract.

1. $\dfrac{3}{8}$
    $-\dfrac{1}{8}$
    ___

2. $\dfrac{7}{12}$
    $-\dfrac{5}{12}$
    ___

3. $\dfrac{5}{6}$
    $-\dfrac{1}{6}$
    ___

4. $\dfrac{6}{7}$
    $-\dfrac{3}{7}$
    ___

5. $\dfrac{11}{12}$
    $-\dfrac{1}{12}$
    ___

6. $\dfrac{9}{10}$
    $-\dfrac{3}{10}$
    ___

7. $\dfrac{4}{5}$
    $-\dfrac{2}{5}$
    ___

8. $\dfrac{2}{3}$
    $-\dfrac{1}{3}$
    ___

9. $\dfrac{3}{4}$
    $-\dfrac{1}{4}$
    ___

10. $\dfrac{11}{12}$
    $-\dfrac{5}{12}$
    ___

11. $\dfrac{10}{11}$
    $-\dfrac{3}{11}$
    ___

12. $\dfrac{13}{16}$
    $-\dfrac{3}{16}$
    ___

☐ I understand how to subtract fractions that are part of the same whole.

To add or subtract fractions when the denominators are the same, you just add or subtract the numerators. The denominators do not change. Try to picture each problem in your head.

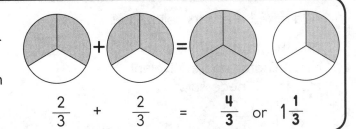

$\dfrac{2}{3}$ + $\dfrac{2}{3}$ = $\dfrac{4}{3}$ or $1\dfrac{1}{3}$

Add or subtract.

1. $\dfrac{2}{6}$
    $-\dfrac{1}{6}$
    _____

2. $\dfrac{3}{4}$
    $+\dfrac{1}{4}$
    _____

3. $\dfrac{6}{8}$
    $-\dfrac{5}{8}$
    _____

4. $\dfrac{10}{12}$
    $+\dfrac{14}{12}$
    _____

5. $\dfrac{4}{5}$
    $+\dfrac{1}{5}$
    _____

6. $\dfrac{7}{8}$
    $+\dfrac{4}{8}$
    _____

7. $\dfrac{9}{11}$
    $+\dfrac{2}{11}$
    _____

8. $\dfrac{4}{7}$
    $+\dfrac{5}{7}$
    _____

9. $\dfrac{3}{10}$
    $+\dfrac{3}{10}$
    _____

10. $\dfrac{4}{9}$
    $+\dfrac{6}{9}$
    _____

11. $\dfrac{8}{12}$
    $-\dfrac{2}{12}$
    _____

12. $\dfrac{5}{13}$
    $+\dfrac{12}{13}$
    _____

☐ I understand how to add and subtract fractions that are part of the same whole.

To add mixed numbers, follow these steps:

1. Find the least common denominator and equivalent fractions if necessary.

$$3\frac{2}{3} \qquad \frac{2 \times 3}{3 \times 3} = \frac{6}{9}$$

$$+\ 2\frac{7}{9} \qquad \frac{7 \times 1}{9 \times 1} = \frac{7}{9}$$

2. Add.

$$3\frac{6}{9}$$
$$+\ 2\frac{7}{9}$$
$$\overline{\quad 5\frac{13}{9}}$$

3. Reduce and regroup if necessary.

$$3\frac{6}{9}$$
$$+\ 2\frac{7}{9}$$
$$\overline{\quad 5\frac{13}{9}} = 6\frac{4}{9}$$

Add.

1.
$$1\frac{1}{5}$$
$$+\ 3\frac{3}{5}$$

2.
$$2\frac{4}{10}$$
$$+\ 7\frac{4}{10}$$

3.
$$5\frac{4}{14}$$
$$+\ 4\frac{5}{14}$$

4.
$$3\frac{3}{10}$$
$$+\ 3\frac{2}{10}$$

5.
$$4\frac{8}{12}$$
$$+\ 6\frac{9}{12}$$

6.
$$1\frac{6}{8}$$
$$+\ 1\frac{5}{8}$$

7.
$$3\frac{6}{9}$$
$$+\ 5\frac{5}{9}$$

8.
$$6\frac{6}{12}$$
$$+\ \ \ \frac{8}{12}$$

9.
$$6\frac{5}{10}$$
$$+\ 6\frac{9}{10}$$

10.
$$1\frac{4}{6}$$
$$+\ 2\frac{5}{6}$$

11.
$$3\frac{9}{15}$$
$$+\ 4\frac{8}{15}$$

12.
$$3\frac{8}{12}$$
$$+\ 2\frac{5}{12}$$

☐ **I can add mixed numbers.**

Rewrite $3\frac{1}{4}$ so that you can subtract.

$$3\frac{1}{4} = 2 + 1\frac{1}{4} = 2\frac{5}{4}$$

$$-1\frac{3}{4} \longrightarrow 1\frac{3}{4}$$

$$1\frac{2}{4} = 1\frac{1}{2}$$

Rewrite $6\frac{2}{9}$ so that you can subtract.

$$6\frac{2}{9} = 5 + 1\frac{2}{9} = 5\frac{11}{9}$$

$$-5\frac{4}{9} \longrightarrow 5\frac{4}{9}$$

$$\frac{7}{9}$$

Subtract.

1. $3\frac{3}{7}$
   $-1\frac{5}{7}$

2. $5\frac{1}{3}$
   $-2\frac{2}{3}$

3. $4\frac{1}{6}$
   $-3\frac{5}{6}$

4. $8\frac{3}{8}$
   $-2\frac{5}{8}$

5. $6\frac{1}{5}$
   $-3\frac{3}{5}$

6. $4\frac{3}{10}$
   $-3\frac{7}{10}$

7. $8\frac{2}{5}$
   $-5\frac{4}{5}$

8. $10\frac{5}{12}$
   $-7\frac{7}{12}$

9. $3\frac{1}{8}$
   $-2\frac{5}{8}$

10. $6\frac{4}{9}$
    $-5\frac{7}{9}$

11. $12\frac{5}{12}$
    $-10\frac{7}{12}$

12. $9\frac{1}{4}$
    $-3\frac{3}{4}$

☐ I can subtract mixed numbers.

Name_____

The students in Mr. King's gym class are completing a 1-mile obstacle course in groups of 4. Each student on the team will complete a part of the course, but they do not have to complete equal parts. Kate, Sarah, Ethan, and James form one of the four-person teams. Read each problem and solve using the information in the table below.

$\frac{1}{8}$ mile	$\frac{2}{8}$ mile	$\frac{1}{8}$ mile	$\frac{1}{8}$ mile	$\frac{3}{8}$ mile
Backwards Run	Skip	Run Through Tires	Crab Walk	Sprint

1. Kate loves to skip, so she has asked her team for that part of the race. How many miles are left for her teammates?

2. Ethan wants to do the crab walk and the sprint, but Sarah says that is not fair. Why do you think that Sarah thinks it is unfair?

3. If Kate skips, Sarah runs backwards, and James runs through tires and completes the crab walk, how many miles, and what events, are left for Ethan?

4. Is it possible for a four-person team to give each person an equal part of the race? Why or why not?

5. In order for each child to complete the same amount, how many miles should each complete? Write an addition equation that supports your answer.

☐ I can break apart a fraction into the sum of smaller fractions with like denominators.
☐ I can solve word problems by adding and subtracting fractions with like denominators.

54

This fraction shows $\frac{5}{3}$. Five-thirds is called an **improper fraction** because the numerator is larger than the denominator. Three-thirds $\left(\frac{3}{3}\right)$ equals 1 whole, so $\frac{5}{3}$ equals 1 whole and $\frac{2}{3}$. One and two-thirds $\left(1\frac{2}{3}\right)$ is called a **mixed number**.

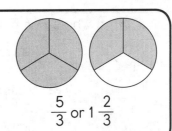

$\frac{5}{3}$ or $1\frac{2}{3}$

Write each fraction as an improper fraction and as a mixed number.

1.

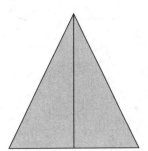

_____ or _____

2.

_____ or _____

3.

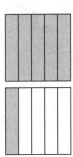

_____ or _____

4.

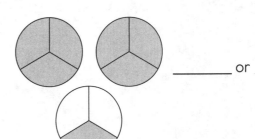

_____ or _____

5.

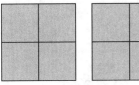

_____ or _____

6.

_____ or _____

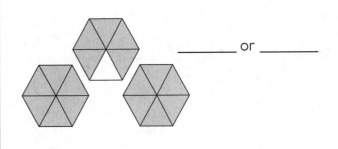

When multiplying a whole number and a fraction, follow these steps:

$$8 \times \frac{3}{8} = \frac{8}{1} \times \frac{3}{8}$$

1. Rewrite the whole number as a fraction. (Write a denominator of 1.)
2. Multiply the numerators.
3. Multiply the denominators.
4. Simplify if possible.

$$= \frac{8 \times 3}{1 \times 8}$$

$$= \frac{24}{8}$$

$$= 3$$

$$\frac{3}{4} \times 6 = \frac{3}{4} \times \frac{6}{1}$$

$$= \frac{3 \times 6}{4 \times 1}$$

$$= \frac{18}{4}$$

$$= 4\frac{2}{4} = 4\frac{1}{2}$$

Solve each problem.

1. $3 \times \frac{2}{3} =$

2. $\frac{4}{5} \times 2 =$

3. $1 \times \frac{6}{7} =$

4. $2 \times \frac{4}{7} =$

5. $\frac{2}{5} \times 6 =$

6. $3 \times \frac{3}{10} =$

7. $9 \times \frac{3}{4} =$

8. $6 \times \frac{3}{10} =$

9. $8 \times \frac{1}{6} =$

10. $2 \times \frac{6}{7} =$

11. $6 \times \frac{1}{10} =$

12. $\frac{3}{8} \times 4 =$

13. $\frac{3}{10} \times 5 =$

14. $5 \times \frac{2}{9} =$

15. $\frac{3}{7} \times 2 =$

16. $\frac{2}{3} \times 4 =$

☐ I can multiply a fraction by a whole number.
☐ I can use my knowledge of fraction multiples to multiply a fraction by a whole number.

Solve each problem.

1. Jacob's class has 24 students. If $\frac{1}{8}$ of them play the piano, how many students in his class play the piano?

2. There are 12 students working in the library. If $\frac{3}{4}$ of them are girls, how many girls are working in the library?

3. Six students are working on math. Two-thirds of them are working on fractions. How many students are working on fractions?

4. There are 20 students at lunch. One-fifth of the students are in the hall. How many students are in the hall?

5. Last night, 18 students read before bed. One-third of them read a comic book. How many students read a comic book?

6. In a class of 24 students, $\frac{7}{8}$ are allowed to attend recess on Friday. How many students will attend recess?

☐ I can multiply a fraction by a whole number.
☐ I can solve word problems by multiplying a fraction by a whole number.

Name_____

A **tenth** is the first digit after the decimal point. It is one part of 10. To find a tenth, count the number of boxes out of 10 that are shaded.

Example: Find the number of tenths in the box.

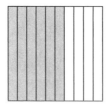

Six-tenths of the box is shaded.

When there are no whole numbers, place a 0 before the decimal point.

The total can be written as 0.6, $\frac{6}{10}$, or $\frac{3}{5}$.

Find the number of tenths in each box. Write the total as a fraction and as a decimal.

1.

Fraction: _____

Decimal: _____

2.

Fraction: _____

Decimal: _____

3.

Fraction: _____

Decimal: _____

4.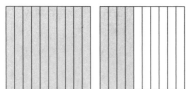

Fraction: _____

Decimal: _____

5.

Fraction: _____

Decimal: _____

6.

Fraction: _____

Decimal: _____

☐ **I can change a fraction with a denominator of 10 or 100 into an equivalent decimal.**

Name_____

To write decimals in word form, write the word "and" as the decimal point.

Example: nine and seven-tenths = 9.7 = $9\frac{7}{10}$

Write the decimal equivalent.

1. three and five-tenths _____

2. six and one-tenth _____

3. eight-tenths _____

4. eight and three-tenths _____

5. three-tenths _____

6. two and one-tenth _____

7. seven-tenths _____

8. twenty and two-tenths _____

9. four-tenths _____

10. seven and two-tenths _____

Write the number word for each decimal.

11. 3.9 _____

12. 2.7 _____

13. 12.8 _____

14. 7.3 _____

15. 0.5 _____

16. 1.1 _____

17. 6.4 _____

18. 2.6 _____

19. 4.2 _____

20 4.4 _____

Write the equivalent fraction or mixed number for each decimal in lowest terms.

21. 0.6 _____

22. 0.5 _____

23. 0.9 _____

24. 0.7 _____

25. 1.2 _____

26. 4.8 _____

☐ I can change a fraction with a denominator of 10 or 100 into an equivalent decimal.

© Carson-Dellosa • CD-104605

A **hundredth** is the second digit after the decimal point. It is one part of 100. To find a hundredth, count the number of boxes out of 100 that are shaded.

Example: Find the number of hundredths in the box.

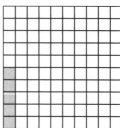

One whole box is shaded and five hundredths of the second box is shaded.

The total can be written as 1.05, $1\frac{5}{100}$, or $1\frac{1}{20}$.

Find the number of hundredths in each box. Write the total as a fraction in lowest terms and as a decimal.

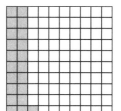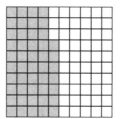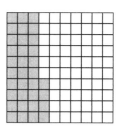

1. Fraction: _____

   Decimal: _____

2. Fraction: _____

   Decimal: _____

3. Fraction: _____

   Decimal: _____

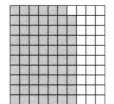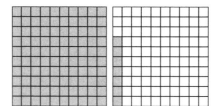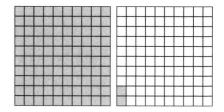

4. Fraction: _____

   Decimal: _____

5. Fraction: _____

   Decimal: _____

6. Fraction: _____

   Decimal: _____

☐ I can change a fraction with a denominator of 10 or 100 into an equivalent decimal.

To write decimals in word form, write the word "and" as the decimal point.

Example: twenty-six and forty-two hundredths = 26.42 = $26\frac{42}{100}$ = $26\frac{21}{50}$

Write the decimal equivalent.

1. nine and sixteen-hundredths _____

2. fourteen and seventy-two hundredths _____

3. two hundred and thirty-four hundredths _____

4. forty-seven and eighty-nine hundredths _____

5. eleven and sixty-two hundredths _____

Write the equivalent fraction or mixed number for each decimal in lowest terms.

6. 0.08 _____   7. 6.09 _____   8. 2.12 _____

9. 0.21 _____   10. 7.34 _____   11. 0.55 _____

12. 16.08 _____   13. 300.24 _____   14. 25.04 _____

15. 600.49 _____   16. 0.72 _____   17. 0.22 _____

18. 25.34 _____   19. 9.09 _____   20. 4.39 _____

☐ I can change a fraction with a denominator of 10 or 100 into an equivalent decimal.

4.NF.7

To order decimals with whole numbers, treat the whole numbers like decimals. For example, whole numbers would be written as 1.0, 2.0, and 3.0. Then, order the numbers. On the number lines below, each mark represents one-tenth.

Write the missing decimals.

1.

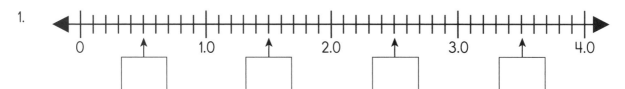

2.

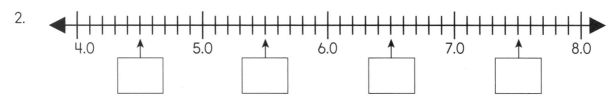

Write the numbers in order from least to greatest.

3.

2	0.5	1	1.5

4.

2.5	1.5	2	3

5.

3	3.5	2.5	0.5

6.

3.5	2.5	5.5	4.5	4

☐ I can compare two decimals to the tenths place.

© Carson-Dellosa • CD-104605

Name_____

To compare decimals, follow these steps:

1. Look at the number of digits to the left of the decimal point. The number with the most digits is greatest.
2. If the number of digits is the same, begin with the first digit on the left. The larger digit is the greater number.
3. If the digits are the same, move to the next place value and find the larger digit.
4. Continue from left to right until you find a digit in the same place value with a greater value.

Example: 0.4 0.2   0.13 0.34

Write > or < to compare each pair of decimals.

1. 0.6 ◯ 0.4   2. 0.1 ◯ 0.5   3. 0.23 ◯ 0.03

4. 0.6 ◯ 0.9   5. 0.06 ◯ 0.60   6. 0.4 ◯ 0.7

7. 0.9 ◯ 0.5   8. 0.7 ◯ 0.6   9. 0.42 ◯ 0.14

10. 0.72 ◯ 0.27   11. 0.25 ◯ 0.52   12. 0.7 ◯ 0.3

13. 1.4 ◯ 1.6   14. 3.5 ◯ 3.7   15. 16.2 ◯ 16.8

☐ I can compare a pair of decimals to the hundredths place.

---

1 pint (pt.) = 2 cups
1 quart (qt.) = 2 pints (pt.)
1 gallon (gal.) = 4 quarts (qt.)
1 pound (lb.) = 16 ounces (oz.)

3 pt. = _____ cups
if 1 pt. = 2 cups
then
3 pt. = (3 × 2) cups = 6 cups
3 pt. = __**6**__ cups

36 qt. = _____ gal.
if 4 qt. = 1 gal.
then
36 qt. = (36 ÷ 4) gal. = 9 gal.
36 qt. = __**9**__ gal.

Circle the best answer.

1. the capacity of a glass   2 cups   2 pt.   2 qt.   2 gal.

2. the capacity of a tub   60 cups   60 pt.   60 qt.   60 gal.

3. the capacity of a sink   2 cups   2 pt.   2 qt.   2 gal.

4. the capacity of a pitcher   2 cups   2 pt.   2 qt.   2 gal.

Convert each measurement.

5. 5 pt. = _____ cups

6. 4 pt. = _____ qt.

7. 2 qt. = _____ pt.

8. 32 oz. = _____ lb.

9. 3 gal. = _____ qt.

10. 8 cups = _____ pt.

11. 5 lb. 8 oz. = _____ oz.

12. 4 pt. 1 cup = _____ cups

13. 4 qt. 1 pt. = _____ pt.

14. 16 qt. = _____ gal.

15. 5 pt. 1 cup = _____ cups

16. 12 pt. = _____ cups

17. 22 pt. = _____ qt.

18. 8 lb. 7 oz. = _____ oz.

19. 14 qt. 1 pt. = _____ pt.

20. 20 cups = _____ pt.

- [ ] I understand the different sizes within a system of measurement.
- [ ] I can find equivalent measurements.

Name_____

4.MD.1, 4.MD.2

> 10 millimeters (mm) = 1 centimeter (cm)
> 100 centimeters (cm) = 1 meter (m)
> 1,000 meters (m) = 1 kilometer (km)

Find the missing numbers.

1. 5 cm = _____ mm

2. 700 cm = _____ m

3. 8,000 m = _____ km

4. 16,000 m = _____ km

5. 60 mm = _____ cm

6. 36 cm = _____ mm

7. 400 cm = _____ m

8. 2 km = _____ m

9. 15 m = _____ cm

10. 90 mm = _____ cm

11. 72 m = _____ cm

12. 4 km = _____ m

13. 9 m = _____ cm

14. 5,000 m = _____ km

15. 84 cm = _____ mm

16. 17 km = _____ m

17. 3 cm = _____ mm

18. 61 m = _____ cm

Answer each question.

19. Penny walks 2 kilometers. Amanda walks 5,000 meters. How many more meters does Amanda walk than Penny? How many meters do they walk altogether?

20. Norman's piece of string measures 15 centimeters. Kayla's piece of string is 200 millimeters. Who has the longest piece of string?

☐ I can find equivalent measurements.
☐ I can solve measurement word problems.

© Carson-Dellosa • CD-104605

> 1 gram (g) = 1,000 milligrams (mg)
>
> 1,000 grams (g) = 1 kilogram (kg)

Find the missing numbers.

1. 3 g = _____ mg

2. 8,000 mg = _____ g

3. 14,000 g = _____ kg

4. 84,000 g = _____ kg

5. 9 g = _____ mg

6. 41,000 g = _____ kg

7. 73 g = _____ mg

8. 57,000 mg = _____ g

9. 25,000 g = _____ kg

10. 7,000 g = _____ kg

11. 12 g = _____ mg

12. 118,000 g = _____ kg

13. 6,000 g = _____ kg

14. 2,000 mg = _____ g

15. 65 g = _____ mg

Answer each question.

16. Megan uses 4,000 milligrams of sugar in her recipe. How many grams of sugar does she use?

17. Harry measures 15 grams of salt. How many milligrams does he measure?

18. Jake's book weighs 2 kilograms. How many grams does his book weigh?

19. Peter's recipe calls for 16,000 milligrams of cocoa. How many grams of cocoa does Peter need?

☐ I can find equivalent measurements.
☐ I can solve measurement word problems.

1 liter (L) = 1,000 milliliters (mL)

Find the missing numbers.

1. 8 L = _____ mL

2. 5,000 mL = _____ L

3. 15 L = _____ mL

4. 48,000 mL = _____ L

5. 4 L = _____ mL

6. 33,000 mL = _____ L

7. 92 L = _____ mL

8. 21 L = _____ mL

9. 7,000 mL = _____ L

10. 6 L = _____ mL

11. 8,000 mL = _____ L

12. 27 L = _____ mL

Answer each question.

13. William measures 18,000 milliliters of milk. How many liters does he measure?

14. Kim drinks $\frac{1}{2}$ of a liter of soda. How many milliliters does she drink?

15. Mark pours 14 liters of juice at the party. How many milliliters of juice does he pour?

16. Isabelle buys 15 2-liter bottles of soda for the party. Her guests drink 18,000 milliliters. How many liters of soda does Isabelle have left over? How many 2-liter bottles does she have left over?

☐ I can find equivalent measurements.
☐ I can solve measurement word problems.

> 1 year (yr.) = 12 months (mo.)
> 24 hours (hrs.) = 1 day
> 7 days = 1 week
> 60 minutes (min.) = 1 hour (hr.)

Find the missing numbers.

1. 24 mo. = _____ yrs.

2. 5 weeks = _____ days

3. 9 yrs. = _____ mo.

4. 14 days = _____ weeks

5. 8 hrs. = _____ min.

6. 49 days = _____ weeks

7. 120 min. = _____ hrs.

8. 60 mo. = _____ yrs.

9. 9 weeks = _____ days

10. 5 hrs. = _____ min.

11. 15 yrs. = _____ mo.

12. 40 hrs. = _____ min.

13. 7 yrs. = _____ mo.

14. 6 weeks = _____ days

15. 240 min. = _____ hrs.

Solve each problem.

16. Gabe spent 4 weeks biking for his vacation. How many days did he spend biking?

17. Ashley went on vacation for 21 days. How many weeks was she gone on vacation?

18. Roberto's flight was 480 minutes long. How many hours did he spend flying?

19. James kept track of the time he spent exercising. He walked on his treadmill for 45 minutes each day. How many hours and minutes did he spend walking after 14 days?

> ☐ I can find equivalent measurements.
> ☐ I can solve measurement word problems.

Name_____

Solve each problem.

1. What time will it be in 2 hours and 15 minutes?

2. What time was it 5 hours and 30 minutes ago?

3. What time was it 3 hours ago?

4. What time will it be in 3 hours and 45 minutes?

5. What time was it 4 hours and 15 minutes ago?

6. What time will it be in 1 hour and 30 minutes?

7. What time was it 2 hours and 30 minutes ago?

8. What time will it be in 6 hours and 15 minutes?

9. Rudy left 25 minutes before his soccer lesson began. If his soccer lesson started at 2:45 pm, what time did Rudy leave?

10. Terrance has 50 minutes left to shop before the mall closes. It is 9:05 pm. What time does the mall close?

11. Amber arrived 15 minutes early for her dentist appointment. If her appointment was scheduled for 7:45 am, what time did Amber arrive at the dentist's office?

12. Carla left the movie at 9:15 pm. She stopped for 30 minutes to eat dinner. Then, it took her 15 minutes to drive home. What time did Carla get home?

☐ I can solve measurement word problems.

Name_____

Kyle and his friends are shopping for their party. Use the shopping list below to solve each problem.

Shopping List

paper plates	$1.49
cups	$2.59
soda (2-liter bottle)	$1.19
napkins	$1.15
cake	$15.45
ice cream	$2.69
candy	$4.75
party favors	$9.25

1. Kyle buys 3 packages of paper plates and 4 packages of cups. How much does he spend altogether?

2. Leslie buys 3 packages of candy. She pays with a $20 bill. How much change does she get back?

3. Kathryn buys 13 2-liter bottles of soda for the party. She only has a $10 bill. How much more money does she need?

4. Nicole buys 5 packages of party favors and 3 packages of candy. How much more does she spend on party favors than candy?

5. Amy sends 135 party invitations. If she spends 15¢ to mail each invitation, how much money does she spend on postage altogether?

6. Pete buys a cake and 2 cartons of ice cream. He has 2 ten-dollar bills, 1 five-dollar bill, and 2 quarters in his wallet. How much will he have left in his wallet after he buys the items for the party?

☐ **I can solve problems involving money.**

70

Name_____

Remember, to find the **perimeter** of a figure, **add** the lengths of all the sides of the figure.

Find the perimeter.

1.

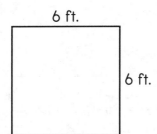

6 ft.

6 ft.

2.

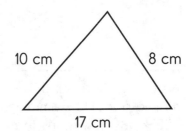

10 cm   8 cm

17 cm

3.

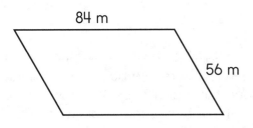

84 m

56 m

4.

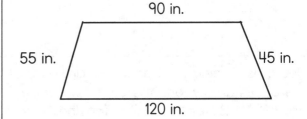

90 in.

55 in.   45 in.

120 in.

Solve each problem.

5. Jeff is making a rectangular picture frame. If the frame is 36" × 24", what is the perimeter of the frame?

6. Lisa needs enough trim to go around the edge of her quilt. If the quilt measures 96" × 72", how many inches of trim will Lisa beed to buy?

7. Greg is building a dog pen. Two of the sides are 45', and the other two sides are 28'. How many feet of fencing will Greg need?

8. Reid is gluing string around the edge of his kite. If the sides measure 12", 16", 14", and 13", how many inches of string does Reid need?

☐ I can use formulas to find the perimeter of rectangles.

Solve each problem. Draw a picture to help you find the answer.

1. Katie is making a planter box out of boards. If her box measures 645" long and 359" wide, how many inches of board will she need?

2. Heather buys a rectangular rug that measures 15' × 38'. What is the perimeter of her rug?

3. Brandon is putting tile around the edge of his swimming pool. His swimming pool measures 55' × 48'. How many feet of tile will Brandon need?

4. Aresia is installing a new countertop in her kitchen. What is the perimeter of the countertop if it measures 144" × 55"?

5. Hector is fencing an area in his yard. Two of the edges are 37' and the other two edges are 69'. If Hector has 225' of fencing, how many extra feet of fencing will Hector have?

6. Hannah is putting a border of wallpaper along the top of her kitchen walls. The lengths of her kitchen walls measure 24', 19', 15' and 32'. How many feet of wallpaper will Hannah need?

7. Sam is making a square flower bed in his yard. What is the perimeter of his flower bed if each edge measures 27 meters?

8. Jessica is finishing her tablecloth and needs enough ribbon to go around the edge. If her square tablecloth measures 72" × 72", how many yards of trim will Lisa need to buy?

☐ I can use formulas to find the perimeter of rectangles.

Name_____

4.MD.3

Remember, to find the **area** of a rectangular figure, **multiply** the length by the width.

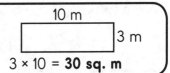

3 × 10 = **30 sq. m**

Find the area of each shape.

1.

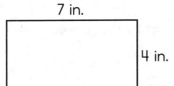

7 in.
4 in.

2.

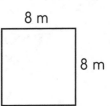

8 m
8 m

3.

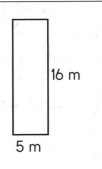

16 m
5 m

4.

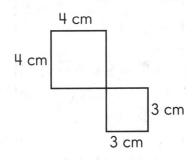

4 cm
4 cm
3 cm
3 cm

Solve each problem.

5. Holly makes a rectangular kite that is 15" × 28". What is the area of Holly's kite?

6. Linden frames a poster that is 25" × 39". What is the area of Linden's poster?

7. If Maria's garden measures 6 yd. × 9 yd, what is the area of her garden?

8. Travis buys a piece of canvas for his project that measures 15' × 33'. What is the area of the canvas?

☐ **I can use formulas to find the area of rectangles.**

© Carson-Dellosa • CD-104605

73

Use the diagram to answer the questions about the Quan family's house.

Second Floor of the Quan Family's House

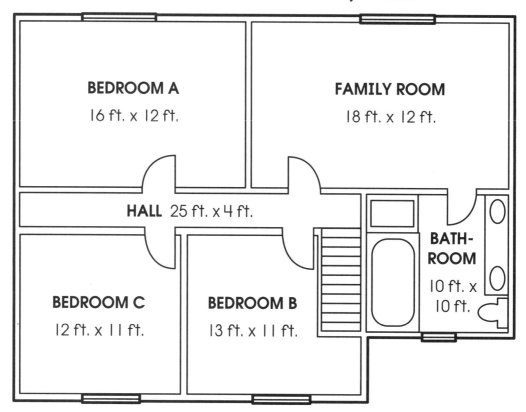

BEDROOM A
16 ft. x 12 ft.

FAMILY ROOM
18 ft. x 12 ft.

HALL 25 ft. x 4 ft.

BATH-ROOM
10 ft. x 10 ft.

BEDROOM C
12 ft. x 11 ft.

BEDROOM B
13 ft. x 11 ft.

1. What is the area of the family room? _____ sq. ft.

2. How much larger in area is the family room than bedroom C? _____ sq. ft.

3. How many square feet do the 3 bedrooms total? _____ sq. ft.

4. What is the area of the bathroom? _____ sq. ft.

5. What is the area of the entire upstairs? _____ sq. ft.

6. What is the difference in area between the largest bedroom and the bathroom? _____ sq. ft.

☐ I can use formulas to find the area of rectangles.

Solve each problem. Remember to write the unit in your answer.

1. Jeremy and his friends are building a clubhouse. The finished size is 16 ft. × 24 ft. How many square feet will their clubhouse be when it is finished?

2. Chloe measures an area of the clubhouse for carpet. The area measures 49 in. × 29 in. How much carpet will Chloe need?

3. Kevin is painting the clubhouse door blue. The door measures 9 ft. × 4 ft. What is the area of the door?

4. Abbie wants to put glass in the window. If her window measures 21 in. × 32 in, what is the area of the glass she will need?

5. Maurice builds a table that is 27 in. wide and 36 in. long. What is the area of his table?

6. Paige makes a tablecloth for the new table. Her tablecloth is 42 in. × 33 in. How many yards and inches of trim will she need to go around the entire edge of the tablecloth?

7. Jeremy wants to plant some grass behind the clubhouse. The area is 17 ft. × 38 ft. One package of grass seed is enough to plant 200 square feet. How many packages of grass seed will Jeremy need to plant the entire area?

8. Ryan and Jeremy are going to paint the outside walls of the clubhouse. Two of the walls measure 24 ft. × 11 ft. The other two walls measure 16 ft. × 11 ft. One gallon of paint will cover 300 square feet. How many gallons of paint will they need?

☐ I can use formulas to find the area and perimeter of rectangles.

The line plot below shows the lengths of some common bugs found in and around houses. Use the data shown in the line plot to answer the questions.

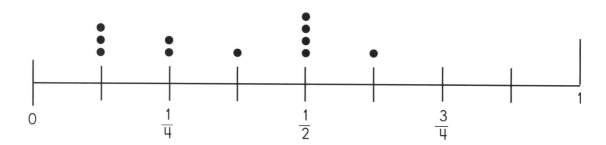

1. What is the difference in length in inches between the longest and shortest bugs?

2. The term **mode** stands for the number that appears most in a data set. Which bug length would be the mode for this data set?

3. Measure the bug below and place an additional X on the line plot for this bug.

4. With the additional data you just entered on the line plot, what is the difference between the longest and shortest bugs?

☐ I can use data from a line plot to solve problems.

Name_____

Use a protractor to measure each angle. Then, identify each angle as acute, right, or obtuse.

1.

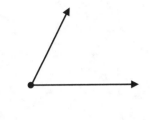

_____°, _____

2.

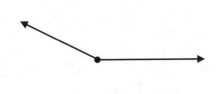

_____°, _____

3.

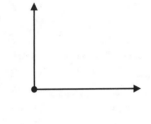

_____°, _____

4.

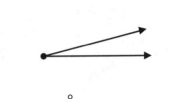

_____°, _____

5.

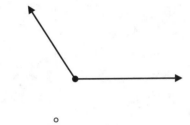

_____°, _____

6.

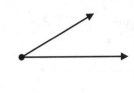

_____°, _____

7.

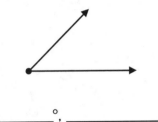

_____°, _____

8.

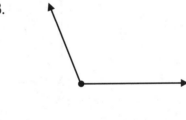

_____°, _____

9.

_____°, _____

Draw an angle with the given measurement.

10. 30 degrees

11. 110 degrees

12. 80 degrees

☐ I can measure angles using a protractor.
☐ I can draw angles with given measurements.

4.MD.7

Calculate the measurement of x.

1.

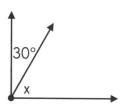

x = _____ °

2.

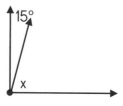

x = _____ °

3.

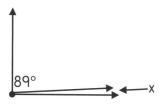

x = _____ °

4.

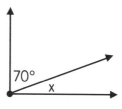

x = _____ °

5.

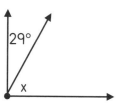

x = _____ °

6.

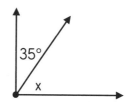

x = _____ °

7.

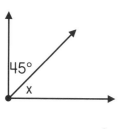

x = _____ °

8.

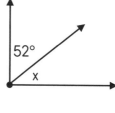

x = _____ °

☐ I understand that the sum of an angle's parts is equal to the whole angle.

© Carson-Dellosa • CD-104605

A **line segment** is a finite portion of a line that contains two endpoints. This figure is named line segment AB.

A **line** is a set of points in a straight path that extends infinitely in two directions. This figure is named line JK.

A **ray** is a portion of a line that extends from one endpoint infinitely in one direction. This figure is named ray ST.

Identify each figure as a line segment, line, or ray.

1.

_____

2.

_____

3.

_____

4.

_____

5.

_____

6.

_____

Name each line segment, line, or ray.

7.

_____

8.

_____

9.

_____

10.

_____

11.

_____

12.

_____

☐ I can identify lines, line segments, and rays.

Name_____

A **line segment** is a finite portion of a line that contains two endpoints. This figure is named $\overline{XY}$.

A **line** is a set of points in a straight path that extends infinitely in two directions. This figure is named $\overleftrightarrow{CD}$.

A **ray** is a portion of a line that extends from one endpoint infinitely in one direction. This figure is named $\overrightarrow{TX}$.

Lines that never cross are called **parallel lines**.

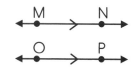

Lines that cross are called **intersecting lines**.

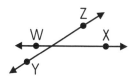

Lines that cross at right angles are called **perpendicular lines**.

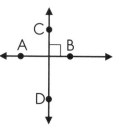

Name each line segment, line, or ray.

1.

_____

2.

_____

3.

_____

4.

_____

5.

_____

6.

_____

7.

_____

8.

_____

9.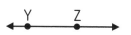

_____

Identify each figure as parallel lines, intersecting lines, or perpendicular lines.

10.

_____

11.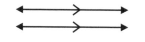

_____

12.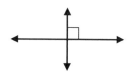

_____

☐ I can identify lines, line segments, rays, perpendicular lines, intersecting lines, and parallel lines.

A **line segment** is a finite portion of a line that contains two endpoints. This figure is named $\overline{AB}$.

A **line** is a set of points in a straight path that extends infinitely in two directions. This figure is named $\overleftrightarrow{CD}$.

A **ray** is a portion of a line that extends from one endpoint infinitely in one direction. This figure is named $\overrightarrow{MN}$.

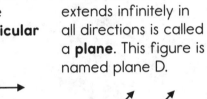

Lines that never cross are called **parallel lines**.

Lines that cross are called **intersecting lines**.

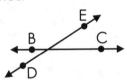

Lines that cross at right angles are called **perpendicular lines**.

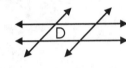

A flat surface that extends infinitely in all directions is called a **plane**. This figure is named plane D.

Name each figure.

1.

_____

2.

_____

3.

_____

Identify each figure as parallel lines, intersecting lines, or perpendicular lines.

4.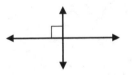

_____

5.

_____

6.

_____

Use the figure to the right to answer each statement. Write *true* or *false*.

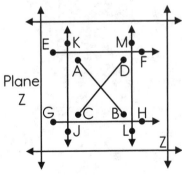

7. _____ The figure is plane W.

8. _____ The "X" is made of rays.

9. _____ $\overleftrightarrow{JK}$ and $\overleftrightarrow{LM}$ are parallel.

10. _____ $\overrightarrow{EF}$ and $\overrightarrow{GH}$ intersect.

☐ I can identify lines, line segments, rays, perpendicular lines, intersecting lines, and parallel lines.

Remember…
Parallel lines never meet.
Perpendicular lines form a right angle where they meet.

Draw a line parallel to each line segment below.

1.

2.

3.

4.

5.

6.

Draw a line perpendicular to each line segment below.

7.

8.

9.

10.

11.

12.

☐ **I can draw and identify perpendicular and parallel lines.**

Name_____

> **Parallel lines** are lines that never intersect.
> **Perpendicular lines** are lines that form right angles where they intersect.

Draw a line parallel to each line segment below.

1.

2.

3.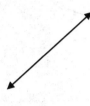

4.

5.

6.

Draw a line perpendicular to each line segment below.

7.

8.

9.

10.

11.

12.

☐ **I can draw and identify perpendicular and parallel lines.**

The point at which two rays meet to form an angle is called a **vertex**. Point N is the vertex.

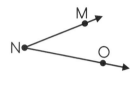

An angle that is less than 90° is called an **acute** angle.

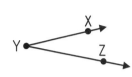

An angle that is 90° is called a **right** angle.

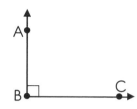

An angle that is greater than 90° is called an **obtuse** angle.

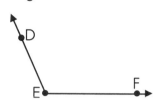

Identify each angle below as either acute, right, or obtuse.

1.
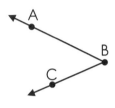

_____

2.
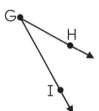

_____

3.

_____

4.
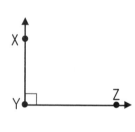

_____

5.
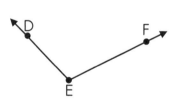

_____

6.
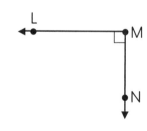

_____

7.
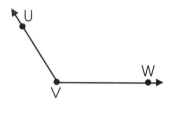

_____

8.
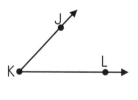

_____

9.
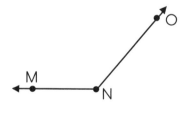

_____

☐ I can identify angles.
☐ I understand how to classify angles based on their size.

The point at which two rays meet to form an angle is called a **vertex**. Point N is the vertex.

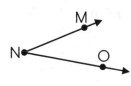

An angle that is less than 90° is called an **acute** angle.

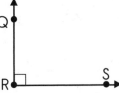

An angle that is 90° is called a **right** angle.

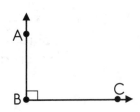

An angle that is greater than 90° is called an **obtuse** angle.

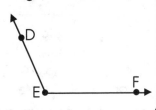

Identify each angle below as either acute, right, or obtuse.

1.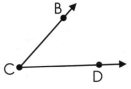

_____

2.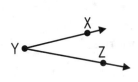

_____

3.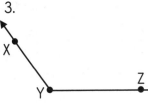

_____

4.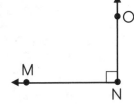

_____

5.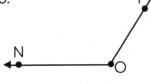

_____

6.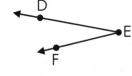

_____

7.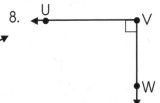

_____

8.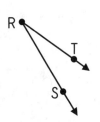

_____

9.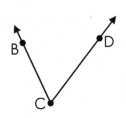

_____

10.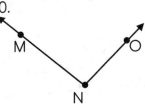

_____

11.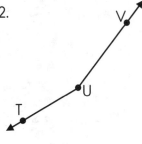

_____

12.

_____

☐ I can identify angles.
☐ I understand how to classify angles based on their size.

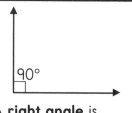 90°

A **right angle** is formed when two lines are perpendicular or form a 90° angle.

An **obtuse angle** is an angle greater than 90°.

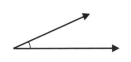

An **acute angle** is an angle less than 90°.

Name the type of angle shown.

1.

_____

2.

_____

3.

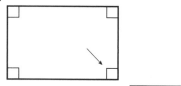

_____

4.

_____

5.

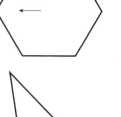

_____

6.

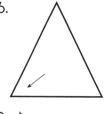

_____

7.

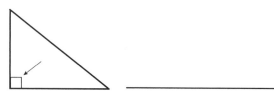

_____

8.

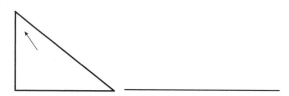

_____

9.

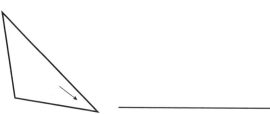

_____

10.

_____

☐ I can identify angles.
☐ I understand how to classify angles based on their size.

> A **scalene** triangle has **0** sides that are equal in length.
> An **isosceles** triangle has **2** sides that are equal in length.
> An **equilateral** triangle has **3** sides that are equal in length.

Identify each triangle as scalene, isosceles, or equilateral..

1.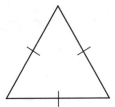

_____

2.

_____

3.

_____

4.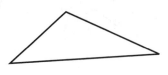

_____

5.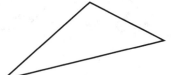

_____

6.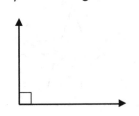

_____

> An **acute** angle **is less than** 90 degrees.
> A **right** angle **equals** 90 degrees.
> An **obtuse** angle **is greater than** 90 degrees.

Identify each angle as acute, right, or obtuse.

7.

_____

8.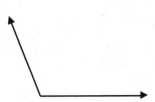

_____

9.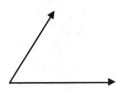

_____

10.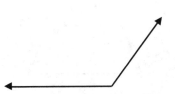

_____

11.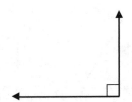

_____

12.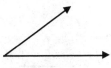

_____

> ☐ I can identify angles.
> ☐ I can classify polygons, such as right triangles, by the types of angles and lines used to form the polygons.

A **line of symmetry** is a line that divides a figure into two matching parts. If a figure has one or more lines of symmetry, the figure is **symmetrical**. These figures are symmetrical.

 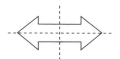

Circle the letter of the symmetrical figure in each row. Then, draw the correct line(s) of symmetry for the other figures.

1. A. 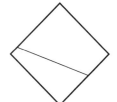 B.  C. 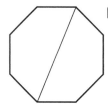 D.

2. A. 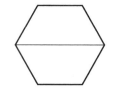 B. 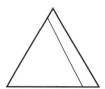 C.   D.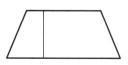

3. A. 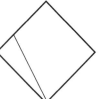 B.  C. 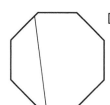 D.

4. A.  B.  C.   D.

☐ I understand that lines of symmetry divide a shape into matching parts.
☐ I can identify symmetrical shapes and draw lines of symmetry.

Name_____

4.G.3

A **line of symmetry** is a line that divides a figure into two matching parts. If a figure has one of more lines of symmetry, the figure is **symmetrical**. These figures are symmetrical.

 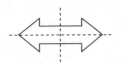

Draw a line of symmetry on each object.

1.

2.

3.

4.

5.

6.
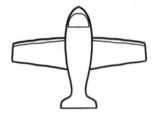

Draw two lines of symmetry on each figure.

7.
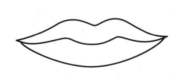

8.

9.
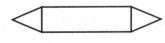

off☐ I understand that lines of symmetry divide a shape into matching parts.
☐ I can identify symmetrical shapes and draw lines of symmetry.

© Carson-Dellosa • CD-104605

89

A **line of symmetry** is a line that divides a figure into two identical parts. If a figure has one or more lines of symmetry, the figure is **symmetrical**. Some figures have many lines of symmetry. These figures are symmetrical.

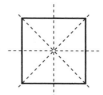

Identify whether each figure is symmetrical by writing *yes* or *no*.

1.
_____

2.
_____

3.
_____

4.
_____

5.
_____

6.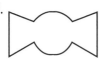
_____

7.
_____

8.
_____

9.
_____

10.
_____

11.
_____

12.
_____

13.
_____

14.
_____

15.
_____

Draw all of the lines of symmetry on each figure.

16.

17.

18.

19.

20.

☐ I understand that lines of symmetry divide a shape into matching parts.
☐ I can identify symmetrical shapes and draw lines of symmetry.

Answer Key

Page 12
1. 5 × 7 = 35, 7 × 5 = 35; 2. 4 × 6 = 24, 6 × 4 = 24; 3. 2 × 9 = 18, 9 × 2 = 18; 4. 5 × 9 = 45; 9 × 5 = 45; 5. 8 × 6 = 48, 6 × 8 = 48; 6. 3 × 8 = 24,8 × 3 = 24; 7. 3 x 9 = 27, 9 x 3 = 27; 8. 6 x 2 = 12, 2 x 6 = 12

Page 13
1. 42 is 6 times as many as 7. 42 is 7 times as many as 6. 2. 8 is 2 times as many as 4. 8 is 4 times as many as 2. 3. 40 is 5 times as many as 8. 40 is 8 times as many as 5. 4. 21 is 3 times as many as 7. 21 is 7 times as many as 3. 5. 36 is 4 times as many as 9. 36 is 9 times as many as 4. 6. 72 is 6 times as many as 12. 72 is 12 times as many as 6. 7. 27 is 3 times as many as 9. 27 is 9 times as many as 3. 8. 20 is 4 times as many as 5. 20 is 5 times as many as 4.

Page 14
1. 6 × 8 = 48; 2. 7 × 4 = 28; 3. 12 × 7 = 84; 4. 5 × 11 = 55; 5. 6 × 9 = 54; 6. 9 × 8 = 72; 7. 9 × 3 = 27; 8. 7 × 9 = 63

Page 15
1. 5, 5; 2. 8, 3; 3. 10, 8; 4. $15, 3, $5

Page 16
2. 5 × 6 = 30 cards; 3. 16 ÷ 2 = 8 pairs of shoes; 4. 8 × 4 = 32 coins; 5. 21 ÷ 3 = 7 rocks

Page 17
Elizabeth, 82; Jacob, 73; Eric, 72; George, 8; Emily, 77; Claire, 24; Demetri, 48

Page 18
1. 6 crayons; 2. $7; 3. 70 books; 4. 3 jelly beans

Page 19
Answers will vary.

Page 20
1. 1, 2, 4, 7, 8, 14, 28, 56; 2. 1, 3, 9, 11, 33, 99; 3. 1, 2, 3, 4, 6, 8, 9, 12, 18, 24, 36, 72; 4. 1, 2, 5, 10, 25, 50

Page 21
1. 1, 2, 3, 4, 6, 8, 12, 24; 2. 1, 2, 3, 4, 6, 6, 9, 12, 18, 36

Page 22
1. 4; 2. 6; 3. 16; 4. 21; 5. 7; 6. 5; 7. 7; 8. 20; 9. 3; 10. 9; 11. 1, 2, 3, 5, 6, 10, 15, 30; 12. 1, 5, 25; 13. 1, 2, 4, 8, 10, 20, 40; 14. 1, 2, 4, 8, 16, 32

Page 23
1. 12, 15, 18, 21; 2. 32, 64, 128, 256; 3. 25, 30, 35, 40; 4. 34, 30, 26, 22; 5. 30, 37, 44, 51; 6. 10,000, 100,000, 1,000,000; 7. 30, 36, 42, 48; 8. 10,12, 14, 16

Page 24

1.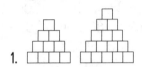

2.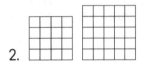

3.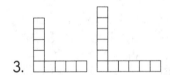

4. Answers will vary. 5. Answers will vary.

Page 25
Answers will vary.

Page 26
1. 29, 37, 46; Rule: +1, +2, +3…; 2. 46, 41, 36; Rule: −5; 3. 16, 16, 32; Rule: ×1, ×2; 4. 236, 246, 492; Rule ×2, +10; 5. 79, 72, 64; Rule: −1, −2, −3…; 6. 50, 53, 106; Rule: +3, ×2; 7. 19, 25, 24; Rule: −1, +6; 8. 339, 329, 987; Rule: ×3, −10; 9. $\frac{5}{4}$, $\frac{11}{8}$, $\frac{3}{2}$; Rule: $+\frac{1}{8}$; 10. 64, 640, 128; Rule ÷5, ×10

Page 27
1. 70 + 7; 2. 300 + 50 + 7; 3. 2,000 + 500 + 60; 4. 400 + 50 + 9; 5. 3,000 + 900 + 10 + 2; 6. 1000 + 3; 7. 80 + 8, 80 is ten times 8; 8. 500 + 50 + 5, 500 is ten times 50, which is ten times 5; 9. 30 + 3, 30 is ten times 3; 10. 200 + 20 + 2, 200 is ten times 20, which is ten times 2

Answer Key

Page 28
1. <; 2. =; 3. <; 4. >; 5. <; 6. <; 7. >; 8. <; 9. >; 10. =; 11. <; 12. <; 13. 1,400,892, 1,408,241, 9,426,597; 14. 328,191, 340,384, 342,192; 15. 65,382, 68,297, 405,495, 929,058; 16. 385,722, 395,024, 409,990, 456,817

Page 29
1. $700; 2. $100; 3. $600; 4. $3,700; 5. $1,700; 6. $900; 7. $1,456,800; 8. $345,200; 9. $250,000

Page 30
1. 70; 2. 60; 3. 10; 4. 60; 5. 80; 6. 20; 7. 50; 8. 30; 9. 300; 10. 900; 11. 600; 12. 400; 13. 800; 14. 700; 15. 700; 16. 200; 17. 1,000; 18. 2,000; 19. 1,000; 20. 4,000; 21. 6,000; 22. 8,000; 23. 10,000; 24. 4,000; 25. 6,000; 26. 20,000; 27. 100,000; 28. 10,000; 29. 200,000; 30. 1,000,000; 31. 200,000

Page 31
1. 41; 2. 35; 3. 60; 4. 28; 5. 81; 6. 94; 7. 111; 8. 132; 9. 171; 10. 121; 11. 412; 12. 640; 13. 271; 14. 332; 15. 756; 16. 108; 17. 144; 18. 220; 19. 174; 20. 225; 21. 28; 22. 39; 23. 47; 24. 18; 25. 17; 26. 534; 27. 332; 28. 133; 29. 418; 30. 236; 31. 561; 32. 627; 33. 857; 34. 161; 35. 459

Page 32
1. 39 reptiles; 2. 77 pictures; 3. 802 pounds; 4. 1,236 pounds; 5. 81 reptiles; 6. 929 people; 7. 170 cages; 8. 262 feet

Page 33
1. 595; 2. 606; 3. 416; 4. 3,934; 5. 7,505; 6. 4,895; 7. 8,258; 8. 5,736; 9. 6,338; 10. 35,298; 11. 177; 12. 158; 13. 146; 14. 466; 15. 19,287; 16. 495; 17. 828; 18. 395; 19. 1,389; 20. 14,538; 21. 412; 22. 172; 23. 183; 24. 346; 25. 221; 26. 1,602; 27. 2,157; 28. 2,849; 29. 30,646; 30. 49,218

Page 34
1. 434 black ants; 2. 1,292 pounds; 3. 553 feet; 4. 1,078 butterflies; 5. 46,084 insects; 6. 10,176 birds; 7. 1,785 insects; 8. 957 monarch butterflies

Page 35
1. 105; 2. 96; 3. 88; 4. 82; 5. 26; 6. 68; 7. 38; 8. 72; 9. 70; 10. 94; 11. 144; 12. 108; 13. 216; 14. 162; 15. 114; 16. 581; 17. 152; 18. 260; 19. 738; 20. 371; 21. 194; 22. 196; 23. 232; 24. 380; 25. 465; 26. 444; 27. 595; 28. 177; 29. 372; 30. 188; 31. 462; 32. 366; 33. 644; 34. 840; 35. 824; 36. 360; 37. 354; 38. 436; 39. 916; 40. 814; 41. 705; 42. 692; 43. 368; 44. 984; 45. 1,168; 46. 706; 47. 1,524; 48. 1,386; 49. 2,628; 50. 1,488; 51. 2,140; 52. 2,613; 53. 3,976; 54. 2,436

Page 36
1. 3,372 miles; 2. 3,215 miles; 3. 2,241 miles; 4. 3,156 miles; 5. 2,082 miles; 6. 815 miles; 7. 455 miles; 8. Paul drove 2,368 miles. Tony drove 2,911 miles.

Page 37
1. 74; 2. 444; 3. 256; 4. 2,176; 5. 72; 6. 1,992; 7. 312; 8. 768; 9. 264; 10. 414; 11. 1,768; 12. 1,032; 13. 408; 14. 1,271; 15. 345; 16. 714; 17. 689; 18. 204; 19. 1,302; 20. 350; 21. 800; 22. 357; 23. 385; 24. 338; 25. 870; 26. 1,088; 27. 4,200; 28. 1,005; 29. 2,173; 30. 1,197

Page 38
1. 703 people; 2. 336 people; 3. 570 minutes; 4. 360 seeds; 5. 5,922 square feet; 6. 150,000 sheets; 7. 1,380 ants

Page 39
1. 19; 2. 30r1; 3. 17r1; 4. 8r2; 5. 17r1; 6. 12r1; 7. 24r1; 8. 8r2; 9. 5r3; 10. 15r4; 11. 78; 12. 84r2; 13. 165r2; 14. 101r2; 15. 338r1; 16. 92r5; 17. 108r1; 18. 47; 19. 203r1; 20. 27; 21. 92; 22. 91; 23. 27; 24. 63; 25. 67r1

Page 40
1. 15 snakes; 2. 79 pounds; 3. 83 pounds; 4. 210 people; 5. 13 customers; 6. 15 pounds, 5 pounds left over; 7. 260 people; 8. 63 pounds

Page 41
1. 82r5; 2. 64; 3. 51r2; 4. 46r4; 5. 113; 6. 503r1; 7. 2,812r1; 8. 692; 9. 1,022r3; 10. 441r3; 11. 564r6; 12. 936r2; 13. 1895r4; 14. 2,118; 15. 2,293; 16. 3,335r1; 17. 856; 18. 432; 19. 1,893r1; 20. 439r1

Answer Key

Page 42

1. 215 cartons; 2. 801 boxes; 3. 1,330 packages, 5 seeds left over; 4. 811 bottles; 5. 48 boxes; 6. 405 vases, 2 flowers left over; 7. 398 bottles; 8. 306 packages, 1 piece left over

Page 43

1. $\frac{2}{6} = \frac{1}{3}$; 2. $\frac{1}{4} = \frac{2}{8}$; 3. $\frac{1}{2} = \frac{3}{6}$; 4. $\frac{3}{4} = \frac{6}{8}$; 5. $\frac{2}{2} = 1$; 6. $\frac{3}{7} = \frac{6}{14}$; 7. $\frac{1}{5} = \frac{2}{10}$; 8. $\frac{1}{6} = \frac{2}{12}$; 9. $\frac{8}{8} = 1$; 10. $\frac{1}{3} = \frac{3}{9}$; 11. $\frac{2}{4} = \frac{8}{16}$; 12. $\frac{1}{4} = \frac{3}{12}$

Page 44

1. $\frac{4}{8}$; 2. $\frac{3}{6}$; 3. $\frac{2}{6}$; 4. $\frac{8}{16}$; 5. 12; 6. 3; 7. 10; 8. 12; 9. 1; 10. 6

Page 45

1. $\frac{40}{100} + \frac{8}{100} = \frac{48}{100}$; 2. $\frac{3}{100} + \frac{70}{100} = \frac{73}{100}$; 3. $\frac{1}{100} + \frac{90}{100} = \frac{91}{100}$; 4. $\frac{30}{100} + \frac{7}{100} = \frac{37}{100}$; 5. $\frac{9}{100} + \frac{90}{100} = \frac{99}{100}$; 6. $\frac{110}{100} + \frac{11}{100} = \frac{121}{100}$; 7. $\frac{2}{100} + \frac{30}{100} = \frac{32}{100}$; 8. $\frac{50}{100} + \frac{7}{100} = \frac{57}{100}$; 9. $\frac{20}{100} + \frac{3}{100} + \frac{10}{100} = \frac{33}{100}$; 10. $\frac{50}{100} + \frac{7}{100} + \frac{5}{100} = \frac{62}{100}$

Page 46

1. $\frac{1}{3} < \frac{2}{3}$; 2. $\frac{1}{4} = \frac{2}{8}$; 3. $\frac{3}{8} < \frac{1}{2}$; 4. $\frac{1}{3} = \frac{2}{6}$; 5. $\frac{3}{4} > \frac{2}{4}$; 6. $\frac{1}{2} = \frac{2}{4}$

Page 47

1. >; 2. >; 3. >; 4. =; 5. >; 6. <; 7. >; 8. >; 9. <; 10. =; 11. =; 12. <; 13. <; 14. <; 15. = 16. <

Page 48

1. >; 2. <; 3. >; 4. =; 5. <; 6. >; 7. =; 8. <; 9. <; 10. <; 11. <; 12. >; 13. <; 14. =; 15. >

Page 49

1. $\frac{3}{4}$; 2. $\frac{1}{4}$; 3. $\frac{4}{5}$; 4. $\frac{9}{10}$; 5. $\frac{1}{4}$; 6. $\frac{3}{5}$; 7. $\frac{8}{9}$; 8. $\frac{1}{3}$; 9. $\frac{2}{5}$; 10. $\frac{4}{5}$; 11. $\frac{2}{5}$; 12. $\frac{1}{5}$

Page 50

1. $\frac{1}{4}$; 2. $\frac{1}{6}$; 3. $\frac{2}{3}$; 4. $\frac{3}{7}$; 5. $\frac{5}{6}$; 6. $\frac{3}{5}$; 7. $\frac{2}{5}$; 8. $\frac{1}{3}$; 9. $\frac{1}{2}$; 10. $\frac{1}{2}$; 11. $\frac{7}{11}$; 12. $\frac{5}{8}$

Page 51

1. $\frac{1}{6}$; 2. $\frac{4}{4}$ or 1; 3. $\frac{1}{8}$; 4. $\frac{24}{12}$ or 2; 5. $\frac{5}{5}$ or 1; 6. $\frac{11}{8}$ or $1\frac{3}{8}$; 7. $\frac{11}{11}$ or 1; 8. $\frac{9}{7}$ or $1\frac{2}{7}$; 9. $\frac{3}{5}$; 10. $\frac{10}{9}$ or $1\frac{1}{9}$; 11. $\frac{1}{2}$; 12. $\frac{17}{13}$ or $1\frac{4}{13}$

Page 52

1. $4\frac{4}{5}$; 2. $9\frac{4}{5}$; 3. $9\frac{9}{14}$; 4. $6\frac{1}{2}$; 5. $11\frac{5}{12}$; 6. $3\frac{3}{8}$; 7. $9\frac{2}{9}$; 8. $7\frac{1}{6}$; 9. $13\frac{2}{5}$; 10. $4\frac{1}{2}$; 11. $8\frac{2}{15}$; 12. $6\frac{1}{12}$

Page 53

1. $1\frac{5}{7}$; 2. $2\frac{2}{3}$; 3. $\frac{2}{6}$ or $\frac{1}{3}$; 4. $5\frac{6}{8}$ or $5\frac{3}{4}$; 5. $2\frac{3}{5}$; 6. $\frac{6}{10}$ or $\frac{3}{5}$; 7. $2\frac{3}{5}$; 8. $2\frac{10}{12}$ or $2\frac{5}{6}$; 9. $\frac{4}{8}$ or $\frac{1}{2}$; 10. $\frac{6}{9}$ or $\frac{2}{3}$; 11. $1\frac{10}{12}$ or $1\frac{5}{6}$; 12. $5\frac{2}{4}$ $5\frac{1}{2}$

Page 54

1. $\frac{6}{8}$ or $\frac{3}{4}$ mile; 2. Answers may vary but may include that it is $\frac{4}{8}$, or half of the race. 3. $\frac{3}{8}$, sprint; 4. Answers will vary. 5. Answers will vary.

Page 55

1. $\frac{2}{2}$ or 1; 2. $\frac{11}{6}$ or $1\frac{5}{6}$; 3. $\frac{6}{5}$ or $1\frac{1}{5}$; 4. $\frac{7}{3}$ or $2\frac{1}{3}$; 5. $\frac{11}{4}$ or $2\frac{3}{4}$; 6. $\frac{17}{6}$ or $2\frac{5}{6}$

Answer Key

Page 56

1. 2; 2. $1\frac{3}{5}$; 3. $\frac{6}{7}$; 4. $1\frac{1}{7}$; 5. $2\frac{2}{5}$; 6. $\frac{9}{10}$; 7. $6\frac{3}{5}$; 8. $1\frac{4}{5}$; 9. 1 $\frac{1}{3}$; 10. $1\frac{5}{7}$; 11. $\frac{3}{5}$; 12. $1\frac{1}{2}$; 13. $1\frac{1}{2}$; 14. $1\frac{1}{9}$; 15. $\frac{6}{7}$; 16. $2\frac{2}{3}$

Page 57

1. 3 students; 2. 9 girls; 3. 4 students; 4. 4 students; 5. 6 students; 6. 21 students

Page 58

1. $\frac{4}{10}$, 0.4; 2. $\frac{2}{10}$, 0.2; 3. $\frac{5}{10}$, 0.5; 4. $1\frac{4}{10}$, 1.4; 5. $1\frac{1}{10}$, 1.1; 6. $1\frac{9}{10}$, 1.9

Page 59

1. 3.5; 2. 6.1; 3. 0.8; 4. 8.3; 5. 0.3; 6. 2.1; 7. 0.7; 8. 20.2; 9. 0.4; 10. 7.2; 11. three and nine-tenths; 12. two and seven-tenths; 13. twelve and eight-tenths; 14. seven and three-tenths; 15. five-tenths; 16. one and one-tenth; 17. six and four-tenths; 18. two and six-tenths; 19. four and two-tenths; 20. four and four-tenths;

21. $\frac{3}{5}$; 22. $\frac{1}{2}$; 23. $\frac{9}{10}$; 24. $\frac{7}{10}$; 25. $1\frac{1}{5}$; 26. $4\frac{4}{5}$

Page 60

1. $\frac{21}{100}$, 0.21; 2. $\frac{47}{100}$, 0.47; 3. $\frac{34}{100}$, 0.34; 4. $\frac{69}{100}$, 0.69; 5. $1\frac{7}{100}$, 1.07; 6. $1\frac{2}{100}$, 1.02

Page 61

1. 9.16; 2. 14.72; 3. 200.34; 4. 47.89; 5. 11.62; 6. $\frac{2}{25}$; 7. 6 $\frac{9}{100}$; 8. 2 $\frac{3}{25}$; 9. $\frac{21}{100}$; 10. 7 $\frac{17}{50}$; 11. $\frac{11}{20}$; 12. 16 $\frac{2}{25}$; 13. 300 $\frac{6}{25}$; 14. 25 $\frac{1}{25}$; 15. 600 $\frac{49}{100}$; 16. $\frac{18}{25}$; 17. $\frac{11}{50}$; 18. 25 $\frac{17}{50}$; 19. 9 $\frac{9}{100}$; 20. 4 $\frac{39}{100}$

Page 62

1. 0.5, 1.5, 2.5, 3.5; 2. 4.5, 5.5, 6.5, 7.5; 3. 0.5, 1, 1.5, 2; 4. 1.5, 2, 2.5, 3; 5. 0.5, 2.5, 3, 3.5; 6. 2.5, 3.5, 4, 4.5, 5.5

Page 63

1. >; 2. <; 3. >; 4. <; 5. <; 6. <; 7. >; 8. >; 9. >; 10. >; 11. <; 12. >; 13. <; 14. <; 15. <

Page 64

1. 2 cups; 2. 60 gallons; 3. 2 gallons; 4. 2 quarts; 5. 10; 6. 2; 7. 4; 8. 2; 9. 12; 10. 4; 11. 88; 12. 9; 13. 9; 14. 4; 15. 11; 16. 24; 17. 11; 18. 135; 19. 29; 20. 10

Page 65

1. 50; 2. 7; 3. 8; 4. 16; 5. 6; 6. 360; 7. 4; 8. 2,000; 9. 1,500; 10. 9; 11. 7,200; 12. 4,000; 13. 900; 14. 5; 15. 840; 16. 17,000; 17. 30; 18. 6,100; 19. 3,000 meters, 7,000 meters; 20. Kayla

Page 66

1. 3,000; 2. 8; 3. 14; 4. 84; 5. 9,000; 6. 41; 7. 73,000; 8. 57; 9. 25; 10. 7; 11. 12,000; 12. 118; 13. 6; 14. 2; 15. 65,000; 16. 4 grams; 17. 15,000 milligrams; 18. 2,000 grams; 19. 16 grams

Page 67

1. 8,000; 2. 5; 3. 15,000; 4. 48; 5. 4,000; 6. 33; 7. 92,000; 8. 21,000; 9. 7; 10. 6,000; 11. 8; 12. 27,000; 13. 18 liters; 14. 500 milliliters; 15. 14,000 milliliters; 16. 12 liters, 6 bottles

Page 68

1. 2; 2. 35; 3. 108; 4. 2; 5. 480; 6. 7; 7. 2; 8. 5; 9. 63; 10. 300; 11. 180; 12. 2,400; 13. 84; 14. 42; 15. 4; 16. 28 days; 17. 3 weeks; 18. 8 hours; 19. 10 hours and 30 minutes

Page 69

1. 8:45; 2. 10:15; 3. 8:15; 4. 10:45; 5. 10:45; 6. 11:45; 7. 12:00; 8. 1:45; 9. 2:20 pm; 10. 9:55 pm; 11. 7:30 am; 12. 10:00 pm

Page 70

1. $14.83; 2. $5.75; 3. $5.47; 4. $32.00; 5. $20.25; 6. $4.67

Page 71

1. 24 feet; 2. 35 centimeters; 3. 280 meters; 4. 310 inches; 5. 120 inches; 6. 336 inches; 7. 146

Answer Key

feet; 8. 55 inches

Page 72
1. 2,008 inches; 2. 106 feet; 3. 206 feet; 4. 398 inches; 5. 13 feet; 6. 90 feet; 7. 108 meters; 8. 8 yards

Page 73
1. 28 square inches; 2. 64 square meters; 3. 80 square meters; 4. 25 square centimeters; 5. 420 square inches; 6. 975 square inches; 7. 54 square yards; 8. 495 square feet

Page 74
1. 216; 2. 84; 3. 467; 4. 100; 5. 883; 6. 92

Page 75
1. 384 square feet; 2. 1,421 square inches; 3. 36 square feet; 4. 672 square inches; 5. 972 square inches; 6. 4 yards, 6 inches; 7. 4 packages; 8. 3 gallons

Page 76
1. $\frac{4}{8}$ or $\frac{1}{2}$ inch; 2. $\frac{1}{2}$ inch; 3. place dot over $\frac{3}{4}$; 4. $\frac{5}{8}$ inch

Page 77
1. 62°, acute; 2. 153°, obtuse; 3. 30°, acute; 4. 14°, acute; 5. 123°, obtuse; 6. 90°, right; 7. 45°, acute; 8. 112°, obtuse; 9. 136°, obtuse; 10-12. Check student work.

Page 78
1. 60; 2. 75; 3. 1; 4. 20; 5. 61; 6. 55; 7. 45; 8. 38

Page 79
1. line segment; 2. line segment; 3. line; 4. ray; 5. line; 6. line segment; 7. ray CD; 8. line RS; 9. ray EF; 10. line segment YZ; 11. line UV; 12. line segment NO

Page 80
1. ray CD; 2. line CM; 3. line segment XY; 4. line AB; 5. line segment BC; 6. line ST; 7. ray EF; 8. ray DE; 9. line YZ; 10. intersecting; 11. parallel; 12. perpendicular

Page 81
1. line MN; 2. ray ST; 3. line segment UV; 4. perpendicular; 5. intersecting; 6. parallel; 7. false; 8. false; 9. true; 10. false

Page 82
Check student work. 1–6. Lines should not touch. 7–12. Lines should form right angles.

Page 83
Check student work. 1–6. Lines should not touch. 7–12. Lines should form right angles.

Page 84
1. acute; 2. acute; 3. obtuse; 4. right; 5. obtuse; 6. right; 7. obtuse; 8. acute; 9. obtuse

Page 85
1. acute; 2. right; 3. obtuse; 4. right; 5. obtuse; 6. acute; 7. obtuse; 8. right; 9. acute; 10. obtuse; 11. acute; 12. obtuse

Page 86
1. acute; 2. right; 3. right; 4. obtuse; 5. obtuse; 6. acute; 7. obtuse; 8. acute; 9. right; 10. acute

Page 87
1. equilateral; 2. isosceles; 3. scalene; 4. scalene; 5. scalene; 6. equilateral; 7. right; 8. obtuse; 9. acute; 10. obtuse; 11. right; 12. acute

page 88
1. C; 2. A; 3. B; 4. B; Check student work.

Page 89

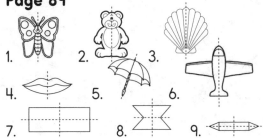

Answer Key

Page 90

1. yes; 2. yes; 3. yes; 4. no; 5. yes; 6. yes; 7. no; 8. no; 9. yes; 10; no; 11. yes; 12. yes; 13. yes; 14. yes; 15. no;

16. 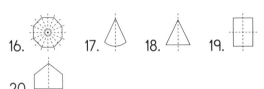 17. 18. 19.

20.